FIGURES IN A
LANDSCAPE

FIGURES IN A LANDSCAPE

A guide to the great historical characters of North Wales

Part Two:
The 18th to 20th centuries

MICHAEL SENIOR

'I think continunally of those who were truly great'
- Stephen Spender

ISBN: 0-86381-488-3

Cover design: Smala, Caernarfon

First published in 2000 by
Gwasg Carreg Gwalch, 12 Iard yr Orsaf, Llanrwst, Wales LL26 0EH
Tel: 01492 642031   Fax: 01492 641502
e-mail: books@carreg-gwalch.co.uk   Internet: www.carreg-gwalch.co.uk

Contents

Introduction 6

Madocks 9

The First Marquess of Anglesey 37

Lloyd George 64

Clough Williams-Ellis 98

Epilogue..120

INTRODUCTION TO PART TWO

The themes running through the first half of this book included those of lineage and inheritance. The latter was in many ways problematic. Some of those who succeeded in making it to the top of the historical scale did so by breaking through the constricting mould of the Welsh inheritance system, either by ousting their siblings or through the adoption of the Norman system of primogeniture – while at the same time retaining the rights which went with the status of lineage, reinforced and promoted by judicious marriage.

After the middle of the sixteenth century such factors no longer applied. You could come from anywhere, and be anybody, and by your own force of energy and determination, backed up, of course, by wealth, succeed in gaining a position of power.

This is the main issue of difference between the figures in the first and second halves of this story. But there are others, some of them more subtle.

We saw that the Wynns were capable of operating in foreign countries, and that their professional life involved being in London, for instance at court; and we remarked that this was a trend which would accelerate. What increased greatly in the century after their time was the scale of the amount of coming and going. Madocks, for instance, was active in three distant places – London, Lincolnshire, and North Wales – at the same time. It is hardly surprising that the theme of the need for improved roads lies in the background of his schemes.

With greater mobility came the opening up of markets and opportunities for the exploitation of North Wales' raw materials – again a trend initiated by the Wynn family. North Wales became increasingly a part of the network of the new commercial world. In doing so it accepted a shift from its simple agricultural economy towards a slightly more urban one. Thus the land itself changed. In place of the scattered farmsteads of a pastoral society towns began to develop, in the later eighteenth century, near to the mines and quarries and around the ports. Previously the medieval castle-boroughs were the only towns the area knew.

What is perhaps surprising is that throughout this period of change North Wales retained the indomitable Welshness of its culture and traditions. Increasingly this became underpinned by Non-Conformism, and the Capel plays as prominent a part in the region's thinking as it does in physical form in its townscapes.

It is perhaps this resilience at its roots which enabled North Wales to accept the importation of skills and systems without being overcome by them. At the same time, remarkably, the old squirearchy personified by the Wynns retained its status and its lands, a tribute no doubt to its own adaptability.

One of the features of the second half of this story is its remarkable social mix. This, I feel, is characteristic not just of the time but of the place. Whatever may be the case elsewhere, patrician and plebeian can gain equal prominence in history in North Wales.

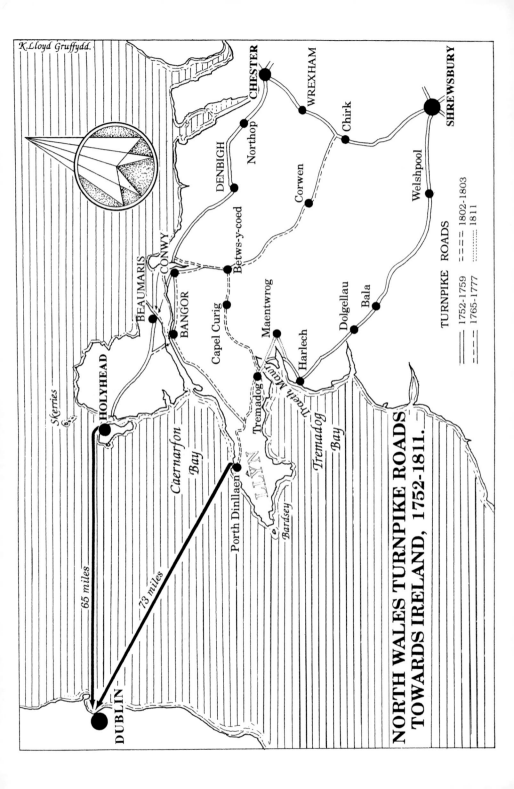

K.Lloyd Gruffydd.

**NORTH WALES TURNPIKE ROADS
TOWARDS IRELAND, 1752-1811.**

TURNPIKE ROADS

———— 1752-1759 ===== 1802-1803
– – – – 1765-1777 ············· 1811

CHESTER

WREXHAM

Chirk

SHREWSBURY

Northop

DENBIGH

Corwen

Welshpool

Betws-y-coed

CONWY

BEAUMARIS

BANGOR

Capel Curig

Maentwrog

Dolgellau

Bala

Harlech

Traeth Mawr

HOLYHEAD

Skerries

Caernarfon Bay

Tremadog

Tremadog Bay

LLYN

Porth Dinllaen

Bardsey

65 miles

73 miles

DUBLIN

Madocks

'The Age of Revolutions' is a convenient phrase which highlights one characteristic of the end of the eighteenth century: that it was a time of radical change. Although we should always bear in mind that the three revolutions to which it refers, the Industrial, the American and the French, were of very different types, the fact that these all occurred during those (say) thirty years makes us aware that there are, in history, times of great and sudden change. William Alexander Madocks was born just at the start of one of these, in London, on 17th June 1773.

George III was on the throne – indeed, in spite of bouts of madness he was to remain so for most of Madocks' life. Lord North was Prime Minister. Rioting had started in the American colonies the previous year. It was the year of Madocks' birth that matters reached a flashpoint, when opposition to the monopoly granted to the East India Company resulted in the destruction, in Boston harbour, of three cargoes of tea, an apparently insignificant event but probably correctly identified as the starting point of the American War of Independence.

If we regard the Industrial Revolution as having started in the 1760's (Watt patented his first steam engine in 1769), it is perhaps surprising that its social and political effects were not really apparent until early the next century. One such effect (the demand for slate) was to affect Madocks, by a series of coincidences which he could not have foreseen, only at the very end of his career. During the last years of the eighteenth century life in Britain was predominantly rural and agricultural, and until the start of the Napoleonic wars it was generally prosperous. As if in anticipation of the squalor and urbanisation which was just about to take place, a romantic interest in landscape flourished, giving rise among a cultivated and leisured class to wholesale 'improvements' of views and settings represented first by the work of Capability Brown and then, with a change of emphasis towards exaggerating nature rather than controlling it, of Humphrey Repton. Jane Austen, writing in the second decade of the next century, catches the contradiction of a rather mindless fashion for interfering with nature to make it more 'picturesque'. 'It wants improvement, ma'am, beyond any thing,' says Mr Rushworth in 'Mansfield Park'. 'I never saw a place that wanted so much improvement in my life . . . '

Madocks grew up at a time when the wilder parts of Britain were just beginning to be seen in a romantic light. Wordsworth's move to live at Grasmere, in 1799, is a symptom of artistic taste. Turner's tour of the north of England in 1797 is another landmark in the growth of interest in the grandeur of Britain's less tamed landscape. Madocks himself forms, in the end, something of a pivotal point, fundamentally a part of the romantic movement but poised between love of the picturesque and a desire for 'improvement'. We must remember that the blossoming of the romantic period actually overlapped with the start of the age of engineers.

Much concerning him is in fact paradoxical, and the immediate circumstances of his origin exemplify this. He was born into a prosperous professional family in London, his father being a successful barrister who subsequently became a K.C., and in due course moved to Kent. Nothing could be more English. Yet this was at the same time an old Norman-Welsh family of the North Wales border, very much in the style of that of Owain Glyndŵr, descended from a governor of Diserth castle in the time of Henry II and the owners, still, of properties in the Wrexham area, at Gresford and Llangwyfan. He thus had access to two worlds which were perhaps, given his temperament, complementary rather than contradictory: that of the old traditional landowning class of North Wales, and the scene of wealth and power at the hub of metropolitan vitality. William was to keep both these in balance for the rest of his life.

He had two elder brothers, and hence little prospect of a large inheritance, and the scheme seems to have been that he would follow his father's career. He went to Charterhouse, and left suddenly after an unrecorded escapade, the result of which seems to have been that he had a period of training as a solicitor even before going to Oxford early, at the age of sixteen. Pitt the younger was Prime Minister by then. Shortly afterwards the French Revolution took place, and in February 1793 England went to war with France.

During Madocks' youth English cultural taste had largely been conditioned by the habit of taking the Grand Tour. This, a leisurely progress around the great cities of Europe, particularly those with classical connections, brought back, like holiday snapshots, an admiration of Greek and Roman ruins, Palladian villas and romantic landscapes. When it became impossible to travel through France all this came to a sudden halt, and by the time Madocks left Oxford and went to train for the bar at

Lincoln's Inn, attention was firmly focussed on travel within Britain and aesthetic appreciation followed suit. Britain's ruins were of course medieval rather than classical, hence the move towards a love of things Gothic, together with a more romantic attitude to wilderness and weather. Wordsworth and Turner were a part of this. It would have seemed not only natural but culturally correct for Madocks to travel frequently to the family's North Wales property and consider what might be done with it. It is an interesting reflection on his personality that when it actually came to designing things he seems to have kept a firm classical taste, and, as a poignant irony, right at the end of his life he himself took the Grand Tour (Europe now being open again) which he could only have heard about in his youth.

Madocks behaved all his life as if he were a rich man. He was not. When his father died in 1794 he himself was left some land in Denbighshire, in his own right, and a holding in an iron-works at Brymbo. There was indeed some cash, and a holding in stock, both of which amounted to £7000 in all and would have been enough for him to start on his subsequent enterprises, but certainly not to carry them out. Much of the Welsh estate was entailed, to some cousins, although it eventually reverted, presumably to his eldest brother John. Much of his father's money was left in trust. This was a significant amount: £50,000 in annuities. The purpose of the trust was given as the purchase of freehold lands.

It was presumably with this (and therefore as the trust, rather than in his own right) that he bought two small farms and some woodland at Dolmelynllyn, near Dolgellau. Although the other trustees must have seen this as an investment, William clearly saw it as a holiday home, and set about improving it. He carried out landscaping, and constructed a new riverside walk to the nearby waterfall of Rhaeadr-ddu. House parties were not only a fashion of the time but very much in line with Madocks' temperament. It is clear that he was sociable and had a great capacity for enjoyment.

We cannot but be surprised at the amount of travelling that went on in Britain in the late eighteenth century, before the engineers, notably Thomas Telford, speeded up coach travel by levelling and straightening through routes, with works such as bridges, cuttings and viaducts. Madocks at this time was a Fellow of All Souls, though we may suppose this was an honour rather than a job, and he continued his law studies in London. His friends were also mainly southern based. Weekending in North Wales was hardly practical when it took two and a half days to get there, and their holidays at Dolmelynllyn were evidently extended.

11

Nevertheless Madocks travelled backwards and forwards between North Wales and southern and eastern England all his life. This is all the more surprising given the enormous amount he achieved at both ends of these journeys, whole days of which were inevitably spent in coaches. It is also surprising that he should choose this way of life, since he suffered severely from an early age from rheumatism. The enormous exuberance of his correspondence masks almost constant ill-health.

The Napoleonic wars caused serious shortages in Britain, particularly of corn, which affect our present story in a two-edged way. The need for agricultural improvement put up the value of land; and the widespread poverty brought down the cost of labour. It was, in other words, an ideal time to acquire marginal lands, and to make them productive. When Madocks turned his attention to Traeth Mawr, that he should be aware of this area at all is explicable by its landscape fame, and highlights the paradox. It was then at high tide a broad sheet of water in which the greater mountains of Snowdonia were reflected. At low tide it was a vast tract of stream and sand loud with water-birds. Madocks was to change all that. In him, in fact, we see the transition from the romantics to the engineers, the point at which the word 'improvement' lost its picturesque import and took on a financial one.

Madocks had at this point as backing not only his own small properties in Denbighshire, which were increasing in capital value and very probably, with the mania for agricultural improvements spurred by the war, in revenue as well, but also the large fund of which he was one trustee, the purpose of which was to acquire land. This may in effect have underwritten a loan, since the land he acquired was definitely his and not the trust's, and according to Elisabeth Beazley, whose book 'Madocks and the Wonder of Wales' is our best information on any of these details, he borrowed money from his mother. We cannot help being reminded, not for the first or the last time, of Sir John Wynn, whose habit of buying land with borrowed money got him, in the end, into difficulties.

Some small reclamations had already taken place on Traeth Mawr. No doubt those who carried these out, and also Madocks himself, were aware of Sir John Wynn's plan, abandoned following good advice in 1625, to reclaim the whole area of it. Madocks arrived at a time of high ambition, and correspondingly high rewards. What he was eventually to do was to be regarded as a great national effort. He was probably not aware at the time of his arrival at Penmorfa that this was to be so. What he cannot fail to have seen, though, was the scope for carrying out improvements such as would increase significantly the value of the land.

In 1798 a part of the estate of Richard Tavistock of Rhiwlas near Bala

Maddocks' first embankment

Tremadog Town Square

came on the market, and Madocks bought eight small farms fronting the Traeth in the neighbourhood of Penmorfa. Circumstances seemed at once to go his way. The year 1799 was a year of bad harvest.

Madocks now owned both sides of a small inlet in front of Penmorfa on one side of the Traeth, and in 1800 he enclosed it with an embankment. He used the skills of an engineer called John Creasy, from Lincolnshire, who had forty-five years experience of land reclamation. It was not a slight or casual undertaking, and it raised a certain amount of opposition. Two miles of embankment were built, out of sand and turf, some twenty foot high. Flood prevention was part of the justification, a great problem in the low, and fertile, farmland bordering the Traeth. The cost was considerable, even in conditions of cheap labour, amounting to some £2,800 of presumably borrowed money, backed perhaps by the Madocks family Trust. It paid off, and the fact that it did was decisive for Madocks' future and indeed for the results on the structure of North Wales.

This first adventure into engineering secured the reclamation of 1,082 acres. By the next year, 1801, Madocks was growing oats on it, and in the following two years expanded into wheat, rape and barley. He was thus, at a time of agricultural boom and soaring land prices, suddenly rich. His aim was the establishment of permanent pasture, for which the grains were cover crops. In recognition of his enterprise the Board of Agriculture gave him a Gold Medal.

He had bought himself a house here now, an old cottage called Tan yr Allt, which he set about converting into something of a fashionable villa. Although the style is not generally Welsh, the shallow pitch of the roof which gives it its innovatory character was partly dictated by the size of the slates which he obtained from Penrhyn quarry. A steep pitch would not have sustained them. Yet it is this roofline, as much as anything else, which gives the air of repose and its hint of southern Europe. Casement windows instead of sashes were another modern touch.

Madocks became Member of Parliament for Boston in Lincolnshire in 1802, and remained so for eighteen years. Boston was a seaport, and he already had a contact with the area through his engineer John Creasy, but there seems no particular reason for this choice and we must suppose that it was based mainly on the availability of the seat. Once elected, he would not have had to spend a great deal of time in his constituency, but we know that he did take his duty to it seriously. We shall see a little later that he also took seriously his role at Westminster. Given this degree of commitment, and the problems of travelling, it is all the more surprising that his schemes in North Wales grew so ambitious.

When his mother died in 1804 William inherited the Wrexham prop-

The church of Tremadog was considered a fine example of the Gothic Revival style

erty, which he then sold to his eldest brother. He thus now had some capital to invest, and he thought he saw a profitable speculation offering itself in and around his property at Penmorfa.

It is difficult for us to remember that Madocks' whole scheme was based on a complete mistake. Moreover the eventually successful outcome of it was due to several unexpected factors which he could not possibly have foreseen.

From very early times communications in the area had been restricted by the presence of Traeth Mawr. The sands could be crossed at low tide, but there were treacherous patches and even with local guidance you took your life in your hands. A road came down the Aberglaslyn pass, but from the point of its emergence the sands stretched for miles ahead with rapidly increasing width. More clearly to get from Cricieth to Harlech involved the long detour up to Aberglaslyn and back down the other side; in preference to which it was evidently worth the risk of crossing the sands. Pennant writes, in the late eighteenth century: 'From Bedd Kelert I returned to Pont Aberglaslyn; and soon reached Traeth Mawr, a large extent of sands, between the counties of Caernarvon and Meirionedd, of most dangerous passage to strangers, by reason of the tides which flow here with great rapidity. . . The view from the middle of the sands towards Snowdonia, is most extravagantly wild . . . ' – from which it seems that the road along the north side of the Traeth was not adequate either, so that travellers in all directions rode on the sands.

During the second half of the eighteenth century travel became most important as a factor in increasing trade. With the emergence of cities, which followed hard on the first phase of the Industrial Revolution, business communications, particularly in the form of mail, ran more frequently between them. Dublin was a major one, and its links with both the new cities of the north-west, particularly Liverpool, and with London itself, focussed attention on the road system in North Wales.

Whereas the route from Liverpool could conveniently run along the north coast, that from London, having reached Shrewsbury, could head to a coastal port through Welshpool and Dolgellau, and thence down the Mawddach and up the coast – to be confronted with Traeth Mawr. This route gave a powerful argument for siting the official port for Ireland on the Llŷn peninsula, where the natural harbour at Porth Dinllaen had for centuries acted as a main sailing point for Dublin. Only the sands of Traeth Mawr operated against this argument. The case for Porth Dinllaen was strong too if you imagined the London traffic having to get to its only rival, Holyhead: coming from Chester to the river Conwy, it then had the choice between a dangerous and unpopular ferry crossing or a journey through the mountains, followed in either case by another ferry at Bangor obliged to negociate the Straits currents, and yet another crossing to Holyhead itself. The Liverpool traffic could come this way of course – but with only the one ferry, instead of three, or the mountain alternative, if its destination were Porth Dinllaen. Moreover it was reckoned in the 1770's that the Shrewsbury, Dolgellau route to Porth Dinllaen from London was thirty-seven miles shorter than that through Chester to Holyhead.

With the Act of Union between Britain and Ireland the matter became more pressing on a national level. Members of Parliament, from 1801, had to pass frequently between the two centres. It was clear to Madocks that his new lands were potentially on an important route.

So sure was everybody that the harbour must eventually be at Porth Dinllaen, and therefore that the road must come this way, that a number of substantial inns were built (which may still be seen) along the supposed route. There was indeed every reason for confidence. A meeting at the Crown and Anchor, Pwllheli, in June 1802 led to the formation of the Porth Dinllaen Turnpike Trust, by means of which a new road was to be built to form a link to the Capel Curig Turnpike through Aberglaslyn, which would involve solving, somehow, the problem of negociating the Traeth. The Turnpike Trust Act to bring this about was passed in 1803. No doubt Madocks, as member of Parliament, helped to facilitate this. It would, when brought to fruition, radically change the status of the area in which he now had land. It would be nothing short of a communication revolution. The quiet inaccessible backwater would suddenly become the focus of the nation's contact with Ireland. In 1806 the Porth Dinllaen Harbour company was formed, and a bill laid before Parliament which was to empower it to raise £12,000 in shares. A report was commissioned which compared the various options for the institution of an official port for Ireland, evaluating the claims of Liverpool, Caernarfon and Holyhead. Porth Dinllaen emerged as the clear favourite. It had a permanent deep-water bay, whereas Holyhead was more tidal. Waiting for the tide there vessels would lose the advantage of the tide in crossing the channel. As a result of this report the Porth Dinllaen Harbour Company went ahead with the building of a pier while still promoting the Harbour Bill in Parliament. Their confidence was justified. The bill was passed.

It is extremely hard to imagine, now, what things might have been like had this vast delusion become reality. Holyhead is, after all, with all its squalor and drabness, so firmly established as the communications link between Britain (and now the European Union) and Ireland. Getting to Ireland is clearly important business now, and it has been since the rise of Dublin as a city at the end of the eighteenth century. The decision to designate this the main port for Ireland, and consequently to route road and rail lines to it, was not made formally until 1839, and even then it depended on the chairman's casting vote. Long before that of course its use was well established, and in 1810 a Parliamentary sub-committee decided that a proper harbour should be built. This could not have been foreseen by the Porth Dinllaen Harbour Company in 1807, and at that time Holyhead suffered the real disadvantage of the crossing of the Menai Strait. A bridge was proposed in 1810, but it was not until Thomas Telford was appointed to survey the road network in North Wales that a bridge there became inevitable. Telford started to build the Menai bridge in 1819, and it was open in 1826.

We have to remember how different the world was before that. Before the new road network and the new bridges at Conwy and Menai Porth Dinllaen definitely seemed a preferable option. It comes as something of a surprise to us now to learn from the 1807 report that in the first six months of 1804 no less than 656 vessels sailed from there to Ireland – an average of three to four a day. We have to bear in mind as well that the Capel Curig turnpike, formed out of Lord Penrhyn's quarry road in 1802, which eventually became the A5, had firmly established, at that time, the route for the Irish mail as being through Shrewsbury – it was not until it was decided to bridge the Conwy in the 1820's that the Chester mail coach, which could better serve Liverpool and Manchester, came into prominence. The route from Capel Curig down Nant Ffrancon to the ferry at Bangor was no more a rigid factor in the network than an alternative from Capel Curig would have been, coming down Nant Gwynant instead, to Aberglaslyn, and past Penmorfa to Chwilog and Porth Dinllaen. This all helps to explain why Madocks had started to build a new town, at Pentre Gwaelod below his house of Tan yr Allt, by August 1805.

Today Porth Dinllaen consists of a handful of small white cottages tucked into the crook of a broadly curving bay which ends satisfactorily in a protective headland. You come to it down narrow lanes apparently going nowhere, only surprised, perhaps, by the occurrence of a substantial inn all on its own at the prior crossroads, part of a speculation designed to exploit what was to be the new main coach road, now left high and dry by history.

Similarly Tremadog now is a quiet and modest place, its location seeming very much off the beaten track, a strange contrast to its patently intended role as focal posting point on the new arterial road, as witnessed by the names of its two streets, London Street and Dublin Street. In spite of a large amount of outlying new development, some of it quite unsuitable, the town centre has kept its consistent style and the atmosphere of civilised calm which it owes to its spacious layout and its restrained proportions.

It seems Madocks got his designs from architectural books and from his own eye for style. Elisabeth Beazley tells us that a plan was drawn up by the later fashionable landscape gardener and horticultural writer John Claudius Loudon, then in his early twenties, but, she says, this is not what was finally built. The town was in fact marked out with stakes and planned with rough jottings, as is made clear from Madocks' letters from London. He was most of the time away, and these letters, often of enormous length, make detailed specifications as to the layout and design of the town.

In contrast with the picturesque fashion of the romantic period much of Tremadoc (as he called his new town) was built in a strict eighteenth century style. The Town Hall, curiously and perhaps unintentionally slightly off-centre from the approaching main street, built in 1807, is a good example of this. There was, however, imagination as well as conformity within the scheme. In contrast to the firm neo-classical style of the Town Hall, the church is pure Gothic Revival. Its fashionable romantic stance produced much impressed comment at the time. Again we have an almost startling contrast in Peniel Chapel, a tribute to Madocks' broad-mindedness in recognising local Non-Conformity as a valid part of his new community. The chapel, with some eccentricity characteristic of the form of Non-Conformist chapels, is sheer classic style, all pediment and portico. This was finished before the church, with money raised independently, and the great Thomas Charles of Bala officiated at the opening, which was attended by the eccentric folk-dramatist and satirist Twm o'r Nant.

One other notable feature of the new town was the 'Manufactory', now unfortunately much neglected and in dire need of rescue. This large woollen mill, possibly the third of its kind in North Wales, followed the example of Cartwright's invention of the loom and Arkwright's spinning jenny to put to use water power (in this case) for the production of cloth. Water-power dams were constructed in the summer of 1805 on the hill which forms the boundary and backdrop to Tremadog, and the mill opened in 1806. It was supplied with wool from the flourishing sheep walks of the hinterland, land then, as now, ideal for the grazing of sheep. In no time at all it was supplying the army with cloth, which was sent to London by sea. By sea too came in the works of the mill itself, and at the same time supplies for the inn in the new town and for Madocks himself up at Tan yr Allt. We have to remember that he was at the same time a busy M.P. elsewhere, active in the cause of Parliamentary reform. When, suddenly in 1810, the factory is sold, we are reminded too of the puzzle as to how all this is funded.

The church, for instance, cost him £1,200. The whole thing was, it seems, a speculation using borrowed money, dependent on the choice of Porth Dinllaen and the route of the road across the reclaimed land. This would explain why it was necessary to press ahead so fast, and indeed to undertake the further reclamation, plans for which began in 1807, which included the embankment across Traeth Mawr and thus the provision of a route from the south to the new harbour. The fact that the decision to concentrate on Holyhead instead was made in 1810 would explain the sudden selling of the factory in that year. However, much took place in the meantime, and we shall have occasion to consider Madocks' finances again.

He could not have achieved so much, or indeed any of it, on his own. The man who should really get the credit for the series of breath-taking achievements is John Williams, his local agent. Williams was an Anglesey man, from Llanfihangel Ysgeifiog, who had worked as a garden boy for the Earl of Uxbridge (later first Marquess of Anglesey) at Plas Newydd, and possibly came to Madocks as a gardener to work at Tan yr Allt. He was twenty-one when he no doubt became involved in the construction of the first embankment in 1800. Madocks was five years older. The loyalty which Williams was to devote to Madocks' schemes for the whole of the rest of his life cannot be explained in practical terms. For much of the time the whole burden of it fell on Williams, and very often, it is clear, he was desperately underfunded, having to ward off creditors and soft-talk angry unpaid workers. The worry and demands of the vast projects were only matched by the skill and energy he put into them. All this time he was bombarded by detailed instructions from Madocks in London, the reading of which alone would have seemed like a full-time job.

Why did John Williams do it? It seems he was chosen by Madocks, unskilled and unqualified and with no experience but that of gardening, because of some unique quality of temperament or personality, a sort of idealism perhaps such as set apart his employer. It is clear both from the letters and from the events that there was a powerful bond between the two men which could stand the strain of long geographical separation. Only very rarely does Williams appear to show any resentment at the delegation to him of the whole of the worry and effort. He must therefore have felt the cause to be a personal one for him as well; he must have shared Madocks' vision to the full.

It is important, I think, to realise that Madocks' motivation was not

Maddocks' Town Hall was built in the neo-classical style of the previous century

The 'Manufactory', one of the first in Wales, used water power to process wool

egocentric. He was engaged in what he truly believed to be the public good. It had to be paid for, of course, and to raise and invest the money he had to be convinced of a subsequent profit. Many great men grew rich at this time by carrying out major public works. Improvement was the heart of Madocks' motivation.

No doubt he also wanted to be personally remembered. The naming of his new town, and later his new port, is slightly ambiguous evidence of this. He explicitly called them after Prince Madoc (now more correctly spelt Madog), the supposed son of Owain Gwynedd who had led a legendary expedition to America, in the twelfth century. It was supposed (by coincidence) that this expedition had set sail from an island, Ynys Fadog, in the middle of the land – which Madocks had now reclaimed, now to be seen as a hummock in a field near the church. In 1792, that is, eight years before the reclamation, the legend had been given a powerful new boost by an expedition led by John Evans, a Caernarfonshire man, to find Madog's descendants, supposedly living as white American Indians somewhere near the source of the Missouri. This aim of the expedition did not succeed, but interest in America kept the legend firmly alive at the turn of the century and the early decades of the nineteenth. The coincidence of Madocks' arrival in the very same area associated with his near-namesake's departure was one of many such fortunate chances, enabling him, as it did, to commemorate his own name while ostensibly remembering that of the exploring prince.

The town is a worthy memorial to them both. It is built for maximum visible effect, set theatrically against a wall of crag, making use of a long approach to display its main civic facade, the Town Hall and the Inn, and at the same time to give a swift and pleasant surprise as its market square suddenly opens out around one. It is much studied by students of architectural history, design and town planning. Not surprisingly it immediately became a success, and although its long-term role of coaching town anticipated, as we have seen, several factors which never took place, it took up immediately that of regional market town, taking business indeed from nearby rivals.

While Tremadoc was being built Madocks went ahead with the next step. In 1807 he applied for an Act of Parliament to drain the whole of Traeth Mawr by the construction of a one and a half mile embankment. The terms were complicated but would result in his eventual enrichment. The area then consisting of sands would fall to his ownership, and he would possess too a fifth of the revenue from the area which was then marsh. With Tremadoc paying its way in rent on properties let as fast as they were built, he must have felt reasonably confident.

Draining Traeth Mawr, as we have seen, was not a new idea. Sir John Wynn planned to do it in 1625, and it was only Sir Hugh Myddleton's adamant refusal to get involved that dissuaded him. Pennant quotes the correspondence in full. 'There are two washes in Meirionethshire,' writes Sir John, 'whereon some parte of my being lieth, called Traeth Mawr and Traeth Bychan, of a great extent of land . . .' He suggests making an embankment out of brushwood 'which I hear they doe in Lincolnshire, to expel the sea. My skill is little, and my experience none at all in such matters, yet I ever had a desire to further my county in such actions as might be fore their profit, and leave a remembrance of my endeavours . . . ' It is interesting that both the motive of public good and the connection with works in Lincolnshire should recur in Madocks' new scheme. So too did a rather haphazard attitude to money. ' . . . if you do see the thing fit to be undertaken, I am content to adventure a brace of hundred pounds to joyne with you in the worke.' Sir Hugh is more realistic. 'It will hardlie be performed without great stones,' he says, 'and great sums of money to be spent, not hundreds but thousands – and first of all his Majesty's interest must be got.'

In the end it cost Madocks some £160,000, and indeed the first task was to obtain the grant of crown land (the tidal area) through an Act of Parliament. It was to some extent a part of a rising trend in enclosing common land and waste land, at the same time making them productive and bringing them into private ownership. This procedure was not standardised until the general Enclosure Act of 1845, and before that had to be undertaken by individual acts of Parliament.

Madocks perhaps did not anticipate that his grand scheme would meet with opposition. His first Bill failed to get parliamentary consent, but this did not seem to discourage him. With Creasy as his professional adviser he simply went on presenting bills, and succeeded at the third attempt.

With John Williams in charge of three hundred labourers the completion of the embankment took three years, and in 1811 they were celebrating its achievement. A footnote to the 1810 edition of Pennant's 'Tours in Wales' describes the project taking place: ' . . . a vast dyke is forming, which is to extend sixteen hundred yards in length from the shore of Caernarvonshire to that of Meirionedd; one thousand yards were nearly completed in August 1809. This embankment, which is to be twelve yards in breadth at the top, and proportionally wide at its base, is composed of rock and soil brought in small waggons on railways from the land at each extremity.' The editor's note makes it clear that the work had not been without problems. The materials sank, or were washed away, and a foundation of matting made of rushes and secured with stakes had to be invented (presumably by John Williams) to stabilise them. A road, the contemporary note points out, is to pass along the embankment, 'which will not only prove a most useful means of communication, but prevent the frequent loss of lives occasioned by the dangerous passage of the Traeth Mawr.' The editor commends Mr Madocks' taste as exemplified by his 'charming place of residence, Tan yr Allt' and also his 'bold and enterprising spirit' demonstrated by the gigantic works below. 'May he meet the success he so amply merits in an undertaking which combines so much energy, contrivance, and well-applied patriotism!'

It is surprising to learn that while all this was going on Madocks was in fact applying his energy and patriotism elsewhere. Parliament was at this time in dire need of reform: pocket and rotten boroughs ensured that the House of Commons could be largely appointed by the Crown and the Treasury and a handful of powerful individuals. Madocks as a radical was actively involved in the campaign to improve representation and remove corruption. In 1809, for instance, while Williams was struggling with the sinking materials and the staking of the matting foundation, he made an important speech in the House, the effect of which was that the control of rotten boroughs by the Treasury prevented democracy. He played a major part in the promotion of Burdett's Reform Bill. Reform was not his only parliamentary concern at this time. In 1808 he tabled a bill for abolishing coal tax, which however failed in the Lords. All this time Williams was deluged by long and detailed letters. Only occasionally, in all this, does a reference occur to Madocks' frequent crippling attacks of rheumatism.

Labour was not as readily available, during the high period of the Napoleonic wars, as it had been at the turn of the century. Nevertheless the two to three hundred men employed during these years imposed their own problems. Since they came from distant points they had to be housed, and supplies were brought for them from as far away as London. Not for the first or last time we are struck by Madocks' extraordinary ability to borrow money. It seems from later events that the source of much of this was professional money-lenders acting on the security of Tan yr Allt itself. The embankment moreover would not have seemed so much a gamble as a sound investment. Once it was finished revenues from the lands and tolls on the new road would quickly pay back the loans.

Accordingly they celebrated. A large party and horse races were held in September, 1811. On Monday 16th an ox was roasted on the new embankment. On the Tuesday a church service was held, followed by a procession, after which the ox was carved and the races took place. That night there was a ball. On the Wednesday an eisteddfod; races again, and at night a theatrical performance. Tremadoc was coming into its own. In effect it was itself a large stage set, in which Madocks and his friends could play their parts, in an entirely invented, constructed world. It is plain in fact from his letters that he saw the whole set-up, from buildings to their occupants, as a work of art. No doubt it formed a pleasant contrast, as picturesque improvements were designed to do, to the prosaic aspects of the real world which he otherwise inhabited.

On the Thursday they had more races before the formal departures. By the weekend Madocks was left looking at his draining land. It is strange to find that he seemed to have little idea what to do with this large area of silt and sand which he had so painstakingly gained. That winter of 1811 saw the first investigation into its best use. It would of course have to be fully drained. Sluice gates were provided for this in the embankment, and also to take the outflow of the river Glaslyn which of course continued, and still does, to run through it. In any case there was no immediate revenue from the reclamation. It is hard to see how anybody could have thought that there would be. At the start, moreover, the embankment did not succeed entirely in keeping out the sea. It proved to be porous, and salt water ran through it. It was intended that in the course of time sand and shingle thrown up against its outer side would block the holes between its stones. In view of all this it is little wonder that Madocks' numerous creditors became restless.

Perhaps we should pause at this point to put these urgent local matters into perspective. Britain was at war with both France and Spain. Madocks started work on the construction of Tremadoc and had his woollen mill working in the year of the battle of Trafalgar. In the year in which Madocks obtained his Act to drain Traeth Mawr the French were fighting the Russians in Poland, and in the year that construction started the war moved into Portugal and Spain. That summer, as John Williams struggled to accommodate and feed three hundred men, Sir Arthur Welleseley (as the Duke of Wellington then was) sailed to Lisbon. As the gap in the middle of the embankment remained to be filled, in 1810, he prepared for Napoleon's invasion of Portugal. When Madocks and his friends roasted an ox on the completed embankment in the autumn of 1811 the Peninsular War was in a state of deadlock, to be broken by the then Viscount Wellington the next year, 1812.

By the time Wellington won the battle of Salamanca and marched to liberate Madrid, however, things had changed radically for Madocks. In February, 1812, the combination of a high tide and a south-west gale breached the embankment in the middle. The highest tides of the year were due on March 18th, when, if something was not urgently done, the Traeth would have reverted to tidal estuary and all the work, not to say borrowed money, would have been lost.

Oddly, Madocks' personal response was to stay away. He was busy in Parliament steering through the Boston Harbour Bill, on behalf of his consituency. Elisabeth Beazley implies that in fact he stayed away because he was critically in debt. The effect of the disaster was two edged: while the need for cash increased dramatically, at the same time Madocks' credibility was severely diminished.

Some of his debts were local, but some appear to have been acquired in London, further from the scene of the action and where news of the disaster could be avoided for the time being. In fact he wrote to Williams with an unusual display of nerves: 'Do not let any thing be written to England about it, but let us repair it before it is known.' Urgent action was thus needed on the spot, for which Madocks realised local goodwill would be required. Hence he hurriedly paid off some of the many smaller debts which he owed. 'Half a dozen', according to Elisabeth Beazley, between fifty and a hundred pounds, and one four figure one.

Since the embankment and the reclamation were now seen as a matter of regional benefit, all Madocks' neighbours sent help. Farm carts and all available farm hands were provided, and for two weeks Williams had at his disposal 400 men, 222 horses, and sixty-seven carts; some weeks later he had 892 men, and 737 horses. The great landowners of North Wales contributed, Sir Thomas Mostyn sending 151 men and 155 horses, and Lord Bulkeley 50 men. The Earl of Uxbridge, his Anglesey neighbour, who had not at that time yet joined the war, wrote him a sympathetic letter from his house in Chelsea, promising to send help from Parys and Mona mines.

Nevertheless Williams' task was far from easy, and Madocks' credit remained perilously vulnerable. It emerged then that the largest debt he owed was to a lawyer, Samuel Girdlestone, from whom he had borrowed (doubtless on the strength of the future value of the reclaimed land) the significant sum of £30,000. We now, for the first time, begin to understand how these vast schemes had been financed.

Girdlestone had a lien on Madocks' property, and at once took all his chattels. In order to avoid the loss of the land and buildings too an arrangement was drawn up by which his real estate was made over to his brother Joseph and a fellow trustee, his father's clerk at Lincoln's Inn, with Girdlestone however as tenant. This more or less settled the local debts, but the London ones remained.

Still Madocks did not come to Wales. Instead, rather surprisingly, John

Williams went to London. He could only report that rumours of debts hindered the repair work. In his absence there developed something of a comic opera scene at Tremadoc, as lawyers converged on it from London and elsewhere all intending to take possession of Tan yr Allt, which had apparently been given as surety to all and sundry. Of course they found Girdlestone already there. He had been wise to move so fast. Locals also flocked to Tremadoc to find out what was going on, and found there rival notices posted, some saying that Madocks' lands and goods were sequestered, others, nearer the truth, proclaiming that they were now the possession of his brother Joseph and co-trustee, with Girdlestone owning the personal estate and being the tenant of Tan yr Allt.

Madocks, as a Member of Parliament, could not be sent to jail for debt. The best solution, from everybody's point of view, was to repair the bank. Unfortunately the gap continued to get wider, in spite of the enormous amount of work. With both those most closely concerned now absent supervision was left to Tan yr Allt's ex-butler Pace, a cousin of John Williams', now Madocks' clerk. Money arrived from London rarely, however, and at the end of April the men stopped work. It is hardly surprising, since some were actually starving. A boatload of provisions was sent, but as it was liable to be commandeered by creditors it had to be put into someone else's name.

Meanwhile the tides rose again, destroying the bridge which gave access to the centre of the gap. A meeting was held in London with the purpose of launching a fund, the matter being portrayed as a national public work. Back in Wales Girdlestone does not seem to have taken up occupancy of Tan yr Allt, since on 25th June 1812 it was advertised to let. Here begins another bizarre twist to this often strange tale.

Percy Bysshe Shelley was then aged nineteen and not yet famous. He had published some undistinguished juvenilia, as a poet, and already revealed the other main aspect of his character, that of radical thinker, with the publication the year before of his pamplet 'The Necessity of Atheism'. This had got him expelled from Oxford and he retreated to London, where he mixed with the radical set of the time. Among them he had met a school-friend of one of his sisters, Harriet Westbrook, and to rescue her from her strict background, in the spirit of the rebelliousness which was becoming his trademark, he eloped to Scotland with her and they married in Edinburgh in 1811, although she was only sixteen. They tried to set up a radical community in Lynmouth in Devon, but one of the results of Shelley's provocative behaviour seems to be that he always had to keep moving. He now applied for the tenancy of Tan yr Allt.

It is ironic in view of his radicalism and rebelliousness that Shelley let it be generally known that he was expecting to inherit a large sum of money when he came of age. His father was a wealthy landowner and Member of Parliament, but the settlement seems largely to have been in Shelley's imagination, and since he died at the age of thirty he did not even inherit his father's wealth. Girdlestone, whose decision it ultimately was, was not impressed by the credit rating of his prospective tenant. He was under-age and his rash marriage had displeased his family. John Williams, however, saw the chance of gaining funds for the repair of the bank. Madocks also seems to have distrusted Shelley, but their common tendency to radicalism and Shelley's apparent commitment to the cause of the reclamation seem to have won him over. One major factor in the decision to let him have the tenancy of Tan yr Allt is that it seems clear that nobody else wanted it. It was better than letting the house stand empty.

No doubt too it was the tempting offer of in due course funding the repair of the bank which swayed them, since there was no immediate money forthcoming. Indeed the terms seem naïve, in view of Shelley's reputation. He was to have the house at £100 per year, payable when he came of age.

In any case in September 1812 Shelley and Harriet came from Lynmouth to Tremadoc. He was then in the process of writing 'Queen Mab', which he had started that summer and was to finish the following February, when it was privately printed. Shelley's notes to 'Queen Mab', rather than the poem itself, in fact throw considerable light on his thinking at this time, and reveal him to be deeply influenced by Rousseau and the school of French thinkers which intellectually legitimised the French Revolution. Men are by rights equal; God is dead; religion is a fallacy; capitalism unjustly exploits; marriage is an unnatural restriction; the universe is immense. And so on. It is in this spirit of high (not to say naive) idealism that he came to Tremadoc, and it probably helps to explain why he was there.

The close connection between radicalism in politics and romanticism in aesthetics only concerns us here because it helps to explain both Madocks and Shelley. Madocks is regarded as a radical because the Parliamentary reforms which he promoted had revolutionary undertones. Shelley proclaimed his radicalism in his essays and notes. Both were visionary and idealistic. Hence Shelley now threw himself into the campaign to raise funds for the repair of the embankment. He made speeches and toured the area seeking donations. This was, unknown to him, probably not so much of a good thing. There is some suggestion that his character was out of key with the temper of North Wales and that he was not greatly liked. The episode which put an end to this odd phase of Madocks' public works is perhaps a symptom of this dislike.

It is the more intriguing since there is some doubt about what exactly happened, or even if it happened at all. It is sometimes suggested that Shelley either imagined it or made it up. The latter hypothesis rests on the suggestion that, with 'Queen Mab' now finished, he was ready to leave, and having run up debts wished for an excuse to do so abruptly. Such conspiracy theory seems however a little far-fetched. So, on the other hand, does a literal acceptance of the story as told by Shelley. Perhaps a combination of a real event with exaggeration and highly-strung imagination is the best interpretation.

Shelley said that on the night of Friday 26th February 1813 he was in bed at Tan yr Allt when he was disturbed by an intruder downstairs. His reaction was extreme. He came downstairs with two loaded pistols. He said he had loaded them the night before expecting to have need of them, a detail which hints at further complications without giving us a clue as to what they were. A man was leaving through the window towards the shrubbery, and he fired at Shelley but missed. Shelley fired back 'but it flashed in the pan', then knocked him down and they fought on the floor. Shelley then fired his second pistol which he thought wounded him in the shoulder. The man fled, vowing revenge.

Next day a man called Leeson told the shopkeepers of Tremadoc that it was a 'tale of Mr Shelley's to impose upon them, that he might leave the country without paying his bills. This they believed, and none of them attempted to do anything towards his discovery' (as the contemporary record has it). Leeson was apparently hostile to the Shelleys 'because' (Shelley claimed) 'we were determined not to admit him to our house, because we had heard of his character; and from many acts of his we found that he was malignant and cruel to the greatest degree . . .' The matter was never cleared up, and the only fact available is that the Shelleys left for Ireland at once and never came back, leaving in Tremadoc a string of debts and hostile feelings.

The point about this strange business, from our present point of view, is that it made matters worse, not better, for poor Madocks. He had, for one thing, with typical optimism and credulity, built up his hopes for the future of the Traeth on the expectation of Shelley's inheritance. Now he had to confront the added suspicion left by Shelley's debts. The immediate result was increased pressure from his creditors. Girdlestone, ironically, was by now himself in debt, and not being an M.P. was confined for this to Fleet prison. The vast area of marsh remained undrained, the breach in the bank unrepaired, and the outlook seemed hopeless.

Madocks amazingly remained undaunted, though beset by rheumatism and gout. In May 1814 (by which time Napoleon was exiled to Elba) he wrote 'Still in Bed, but I live in hopes . . . ' Hope indeed seems to have been his dominant characteristic.

By then he was aged forty-one. It was during the next year or so that his fortunes began to improve, with the same arbitrariness which had accompanied their decline. Thanks to a loan from his brother Joseph, on the security of property at Tremadoc, he was able to have the estate conveyed back to him. National matters also went through great changes, as Napoleon left Elba in March, and towards the end of April Madocks' neighbour Lord Uxbridge, of Plas Newydd in Anglesey, arrived in Belgium to command the cavalry at the Battle of Waterloo.

Somehow the breach finally got stopped, and the marsh started to drain. The end of the war brought mass unemployment, and the cold winter of 1815-16 was followed by a bad summer, in which the harvest failed. It was a good time to bring new land into production and once again Madocks' optimism seemed justified.

Even he could not have foreseen, though, the full extent of his luck. In the course of completing the draining of the marsh it proved necessary to divert the river Glaslyn. A surprise effect of this was that the river in its new course gouged out a deep pool where it met the sea. At the same time the rise of the slate industry nearby at Blaenau Ffestiniog (which he could also not have foreseen) produced an urgent need for a harbour.

The quarry at Blaenau Ffestiniog was already in existence by the end of the eighteenth century, when it was bought by William Turner and the Casson brothers, a second quarry shortly being developed on behalf of Lord Newborough. It was not until a Mr Holland, a Liverpool slate dealer, leased some land from Mr Oakley of Tan y Bwlch, or perhaps more accurately when, in 1821, his eighteen year old son Samuel arrived to take over the management of an apparently unruly business, that slate mining there began to be serious business.

Holland, of course, came along at exactly the right time. As long as the Industrial Revolution had been based on water power, as in Madocks' mill, it tended to perpetuate a scattered population. To begin with a lot of work was done in workers' homes, or in workshops attached to them. The introduction of steam-powered machinery in the late 1760's was to change that pattern. By 1800 it was becoming common in factories. This required large numbers of people to be in the same place, and led to the depopulation of the countryside and the equivalent building of towns. All countries which had become industrialised in the eighteenth century became urbanised in the early nineteenth. The building of towns took

The river Glaslyn continues to flow through the reclaimed Traeth

Th harbour of Porthmadog occupies an accidentally gouged out basin

place then at a remarkable rate. In the first half of the nineteenth century the percentage of people living in towns of over 20,000 population more than doubled. All these houses had to be roofed. Hence between 1798 and 1825 the price of slates doubled, a powerful incentive to find new sources and open new mines and quarries.

By 1825, largely thanks to Holland's enterprise and energy, Blaenau Ffestiniog was producing 10,000 tons of slate. This, of course, all left the area by sea. In the early days it came down the mountain on the backs of pack ponies, was loaded in the Vale of Ffestiniog into carts, shipped from small quays on the river Dwyryd down to its confluence with the Glaslyn, where, on the tidal sands, deep-water vessels were beached which were to take it to its destinations. Clearly all this had to change, in a rapidly modernising world, and Madocks was perfectly placed to be the unexpecting beneficiary.

Things had changed too in Madocks' always eventful life. In 1818 he had been re-elected as Member for Boston for the fifth time. The same year he met in Bath a rich widow, Mrs Roderick Gwynne, whose husband had died twelve years earlier when she was twenty-one, and whose uncles had left to her mother a reasonable fortune, which, on the death of her two elder brothers, had ended with her. She lived on a family estate at Talgarth, in Breconshire. There, in the spring of 1819, she and William Madocks married.

It would, on the face of it, be easy to be cynical about this. Madocks had shown absolutely no sign of needing a wife until now, and by the age of forty-six one might suppose him to be settled in his way of life. Whether or not this was a spur to his motivation, he now found that his money worries were over.

He lived at Tregunter, now, near Talgarth, with his new family. This consisted of a step-daughter aged eleven and his wife's sister. They all visited Tremadoc in the summer of 1819. The next year Madocks for some reason changed his constituency. He stood for Chippenham in Wiltshire (nowhere near either of his possible homes) and was duly elected. That was the year in which his brother Joseph died, as indeed did George III.

Parliamentary consent was required to build the proposed new harbour, and rather surprisingly the quarry-owners objected. They would be able to reach it by waggon, but since the Ffestiniog quarries were on the south side of the reclaimed land they could, quite rightly, foresee Madocks charging them tolls for using the road across his new embankment.

Nevertheless the Portmadoc Harbour Bill went through, and after some further delay work started in 1821. Under the Act Madocks was to be entitled to dues, and to appoint a Harbour Master. The new harbour, which he funded himself, was clearly to be his best investment yet. The quarry owner Samuel Holland acquired a quay there, and the future of this slate-exporting port was set for the next eighty years. Madocks did not live to see Holland's main contribution to this enterprise, the narrow-gauge railway which was to replace the pack animals and barges from the 1830's. Even without being able to anticipate this, when the new harbour opened for business in 1824 he must have marvelled at his luck. Having made what might have been a costly mistake about the official port for Ireland, he had ended accidentally with tolls and dues from the export of slate.

Although the railway did not come into being until the 1830's, Madocks was a party to the early plans for it in the 1820's. The delay was due to bitter rivalry surrounding the drawing up of plans. Various bills were placed before Parliament, and one which was at the time thrown out, in December 1825, turned out to be the line eventually adopted. This was a scheme by William Provis, Telford's resident engineer on the Menai Bridge, which was also under construction at this time.

While all this was going on Madocks and his then thirty-seven year old wife had a child. This was to be an only daughter, Eliza Anne Ermine. At the same time he continued his vigorous campaign of improvement, now turning attention to the landscaping of his structures at Tremadoc: 'Plant Ivy all round the church', he wrote from Talgarth, 'and Scotch Firs on each side the Gate to Morva Lodge from Towyn.' Indeed he was pre-sumably now running two sizeable properties.

Once again, in the spring of 1826, Madocks takes us completely by surprise. He set off on the Grand Tour. Now that Europe was at peace again France and Italy were opened up to visitors, as they had not been since before Madocks' time. We cannot but be reminded, as he sailed to Le Havre at the end of May in 1826, of John Wynn the younger's ill-fated journey on much the same route in 1614.

By June the Madockses were in Paris; at the end of July they reached Geneva. It was clearly no rushed affair, since they decided to spend the winter in Florence before moving on. Since Madocks was thoroughly used to conducting his affairs by post it would not have seemed strange to him to be running his North Wales business from Italy. Letters in those days took two days to get from North Wales to London, and two weeks between London and Florence. It has been speculated that he stayed away to avoid confronting his outstanding debts, but all the signs are that he was by now quite comfortably off.

Back home John Williams, however, finally grew exasperated, and shocks us by at this late stage threatening to resign. The fact that he could do so then makes us wonder why he had not done so before. Once again we are baffled by Williams' motivation. Madocks did not take the threat of resignation seriously, and wrote back 'I have no personal benefit but have had the fatigue and anxiety for 17 years of keeping all together . . . ' – a somewhat startling claim when we reflect that Madocks was, quite simply, seldom there, whereas Williams was there all the time. To be fair to the circumstances Elisabeth Beazley should have called her book 'Madocks and Williams, and the Wonder of Wales'. But history often fails to take account of henchmen. What lack of clarity, I wonder, would result if it did? All we can do is note them, and leave the footnote to be expanded by someone else.

In any event Williams did not resign, and the flow of letters with instructions continued. In early spring the Madockses moved on to Rome and Naples. There they stayed for a considerable time, Madocks' letters occasionally showing intentions of coming home, but Madocks himself giving no sign of doing so.

That autumn he failed to get re-elected to Parliament, being still absent, and for the first time since 1802 he was no longer an M.P. The following March they were in Rome again, apparently now on the way home. They took it slowly. There is certainly a marked lack of urgency about the whole journey. By September they had only reached Paris. And there unexpectedly Madocks died.

He died on September 15th, aged fifty-five. An air of mystery surrounds the whole thing, giving rise to the rumour in North Wales that he had returned in secret and was living incognito, like Glyndŵr, in the hinterland of Tremadoc. It is not even clear what he died of. Not for the first time Elisabeth Beazley admits bewilderment: 'It is very difficult to account for the fact that Eliza had no memorial erected to her husband . . . ' Nevertheless it is officially confirmed that he was buried on 17th September, 1828, at Père Lachaise cemetery. The stone is now illegible; it is broken and fallen; the grave is obscured by ivy.

Madocks did not live to see the start of steam-powered transport, in 1830, which was to make the quarries of Ffestiniog accessible to the port. He did not live to see the tax removed from slate, in 1831, which made Portmadoc boom. He missed as well the Great Reform Bill of 1832, which brought into being a world more of the kind that he had long fought for. Even so he saw during his lifetime many of his own creations become reality, and Tremadog, the broad fertile plain of Traeth Mawr, and Porthmadog harbour constitute his memorial.

If in the end we are left with the puzzle of why he did it, we must sup-

The railway along Maddocks' cob in due course linked the slate quarries to the port

pose that the answer is simply because he could. He had energy and imagination in superhuman quantities. For anyone else it would have been enough to deal with the problems of his constituency and to take part in the tide of constitutional reform in the national seat of power. But not, apparently, for Madocks.

The First Marquess of Anglesey

Ednyfed Fychan, lieutenant to Llywelyn the Great, married Gwenllian, the daughter of the Lord Rhys of Dinefwr in South Wales. Part of the reward for his service to the Prince and his successor was the grant of lands, and he succeeded in setting up for his family a minor empire of territory in north and south Wales and indeed in England too. Among his many descendants (which virtually included all the major landowning families of Wales) were the Tudors of Penmynydd in Anglesey. Their fortunes however fell into relative decline during the 15th century as a direct result of their support for Owain Glyndŵr.

In the early part of 1406 the French troops which had lent Owain's cause some serious credibility deserted him, and as the year wore on area after area of Wales submitted to the king. Another of Ednyfed Fychan's descendants, Gwilym ap Gruffydd of Penrhyn, near Bangor, chose his moment well. He made peace with Henry IV, deserting Glyndŵr, and as a consequence became the owner of the bulk of Ednyfed's inheritance in North Wales.

Gwilym ap Gruffydd died in 1431, and his descendants, taking the surname Griffith, continued for some centuries to rule their vast estates from Penrhyn. As is the way with leading North Wales families they intermarried with other landowners, so that the great houses of the region were seats of their relatives. Robert Wynn, for instance, uncle of Sir John and builder of Plas Mawr in Conwy, married (the first time) the daughter of Sir William Griffith of Penrhyn.

During the reign of Elizabeth I and well into that of her successor James the see of Bangor was occupied by a popular and influential local bishop, Henry Rowlands. He was succeeded in 1616 by a much more forceful and ambitious churchman from Carmarthenshire, Bishop Lewes Bayly.

Bayly had been chaplain to the Prince of Wales and subsequently to the king himself, when the young prince died. He was a friend of the powerful Duke of Buckingham, a fact which some thought explained his unexpected appointment to the Bangor see. Sir John Wynn of Gwydir, we are not surprised to learn, maintained a long-running feud with him about some land.

'The Bishop of Bangor is as full of malice as possible,' writes Sir John in 1618, 'who, under pretence of profit to the Church, aims at the profit of his own son.' Sir John's doubts as to his character proved well founded. In 1621 he was committed to the Fleet prison accused of taking bribes in his office of magistrate, and in his ecclesiastical court, while at the same time bribing his way to power himself; and of eating meat in Lent. Bayly had powerful friends and good luck, and the case was dropped.

This powerful man not surprisingly married into the local plutocracy. His wife Ann was the daughter of Sir Henry Bagenal, but he in turn was the grandson of Sir Edward Griffith of Penrhyn. Ann Bagenal had inherited, from her Griffith ancestry, property in Anglesey, including the Plas Newydd estate. It is thus that the Bayly family come to be major North Wales landowners, in effect the heirs to the Griffith empire.

Meanwhile, in a world which might never have become connected with this North Wales dynasty, another great family had been coming into being. Henry VIII, like his father, distrusted the old nobility. He feared their capacity for ganging up against the throne. He was determined to rule the realm himself, and not be ruled by his advisers. To this end he promoted, from humble backgrounds, a number of 'new men'. Wolsey himself was the son of a disreputable butcher from Ipswich; Thomas Cromwell was the son of a cloth-worker in Putney; Cranmer came from a modest gentry background, and was set to remain an obscure cleric until he was suddenly promoted in 1529. The remarkable thing about William Paget, who became Henry's Principal Secretary of State in 1543, is that nobody knows for certain what his origins were.

Paget was knighted by 1544, and when the king died in 1547 he came to prominence again as one of the executors of his will, which he read, as Secretary, to Parliament. Edward VI was only ten at the time, and Paget was in a favourable position to continue his advance. Edward made him a baron, in 1549, and when the king died in 1553 Lord Paget was an established figure in the royal council, now by no means one of the 'new men' but a member of the old guard. As was essential then he kept his precarious balance (and with it his head), only faltering slightly once when caught up in the rivalry between Somerset and Northumberland. It was a matter of delicately changing sides when a change of power required it, amid a quarrelsome and competitive court in which private enmities often obscured the greater issues of religion and foreign affairs.

The family probably came from Staffordshire, and Henry VIII had

William Pagot, the 1st Baron, was one of the 'new men' raised to rank by Henry VIII

given him extensive estates there, where he built himself the stately home which was to become the family's seat. Beaudesert (demolished in the 1930's) from then on formed the focus of lands and wealth which kept the Pagets prominent. William, first Baron, had acquired considerable further lands in various parts of the Midlands at the Dissolution of the Monasteries.

When William Paget became the first Baron Paget of Beaudesert, he arranged for the title to be passed, if necessary, through the female line. This highly unusual procedure, for an English peerage, proved irrelevant for some time, since there were plenty of surviving male Pagets. The second and third barons in fact were sons of the first, the fourth the son of the third; and so it went on quite normally until in 1769 the eighth baron died childless and the peerage would in usual circumstances have become extinct.

Some years before this Sir Nicholas Bayly, of Plas Newydd, had married Caroline Paget, the eighth baron's second cousin once removed, a great-granddaughter of the fifth baron. The tortuous route by which the Baylys became Pagets hung on a further improbability. Caroline Paget was already dead when the eighth baron died, and all her son, Henry Bayly, could expect to inherit was the Bayly baronetcy (as it had by now become) and the North Wales lands owned by his father. Instead he found himself, with the childless death of the eighth baron, Lord Paget of Beaudesert.

The combination of the wealth of the two great families made the new Lord Paget a man of some substance, the Griffith empire of North Wales now being put into the shade by the lands of Staffordshire and abbey lands of the Midlands. This was not to be the end of his remarkable luck.

A wealthy landowner in the south-west of England included some terms in his will, which he made in 1752, which have never been explained. He directed that should his own family line die out his lands were to be left to the heir (at the time) of Sir Nicholas Bayly. What was the connection between this gentleman, Peter Walter, and his contemporary Sir Nicholas, or perhaps the latter's wife Caroline Paget, has never been discovered. It was in any case unlikely at the time that the terms of the will would ever take effect. Yet twenty-eight years later the last surviving of Peter Walter's brothers died (as he himself had done) without male issue. Eleven years after succeeding unexpectedly to the Paget fortune the baron found a second one equally unexpectedly heaped upon him. To the Bayly lands in North Wales and Ireland, and the Paget ones in Staffordshire and the Midlands, were added a substantial part of Somerset and Dorset.

Beaudesert in Staffordshire was the original seat of the Paget family

An early view of Plas Newydd, the Welsh seat which the Pagets inherited

This was by no means a nominal inheritance, since some of the land contained minerals, and in particular the Staffordshire property came into its own with the invention of steam-power, since it was a valuable source of coal. The earldom of Uxbridge, which had died out (but had once been in the family), was recreated for him in 1784, so that two titles as well as three estates awaited the future hero of this story.

If it was thus largely by chance that he was born in 1768 into a remarkably substantial background, succession rather than chance may have brought him a natural ability to lead. Both the Pagets and the Baylys had originally appeared from nowhere and risen by strength of character and force of talent. The Griffith family, into which Lewes Bayly married, had a store of leadership ability derived from an older historical source, in fact not just from the great Ednyfed Fychan but through his wife from the early kings of Wales, Hywel Dda, Rhodri Mawr, and indeed back through him to Maelgwn himself. We have remarked before of the habit of the Welsh leaders of marrying their equals, a practical exercise designed explicitly to retain power, territory and wealth, accidentally producing through genetic manipulation a gene-pool which enabled them, as we saw in the first half of this book, to govern North Wales for over a thousand years. This is admittedly a risky exercise, since it could lead to over-breeding, and it has (as perhaps in the case of the 5th Marquess earlier this century) occasionally gone wrong; but it can be seen historically that it has much more frequently gone right. The type of ability embodied in the man who was to become the first Marquess may be at least partly explained by his family history.

Henry William Bayly, as he was when he was born, seems likely to have spent his childhood at his parents' London home. He went to Westminster School (now Henry Paget) in 1777. It was a time when in all spheres of activity momentous events were taking place. Only a year earlier America had declared its independence; Mozart had turned twenty; Adam Smith had published 'The Wealth of Nations', and the first volume of Gibbon's history of the Roman empire had come out. William Madocks, also in London, was three and a half when Paget went to school aged nearly nine. His progress was highly conventional from then on, Westminster being followed by Christ Church, Oxford. He was enough ahead of Madocks to be able to take the Grand Tour before the Revolution and the wars with France. It is ironic, in view of the circumstances which were in due course to propel him to eminence, to find him in the second half of the 1780's travelling through France with the main aim of learning French. The only trouble on the horizon then seemed to be the impending war between the Emperor, in Vienna, and the Turks. Indeed, in the

*Lord Paget, later to be the 1st Marquees, was at this time a Colonel
in the 7th Light Dragoons*

year before the French revolution, Europe seems to have been remarkably at peace. The aristocracy kept open house. Haydn entertained the Prince of Esterhazy in his opulent chateau.

There is little sign, either, that Paget's career was to be a military one, and every sign that it would be political. In 1790, at the age of 22, he became (unopposed) the Member of Parliament for Caernarvon, the same seat which in its earlier form Sir John Wynn had failed to take and which, in its later form, was to become the springboard from which the career of Lloyd George was propelled. Indeed, such is the small world of this book, for a short time, from 1802 to 1804, and again from 1806 to 1812, Lord Paget participated in the same Parliament as William Alexander Madocks.

Paget resigned his seat in 1804, but he was back with Madocks in Parliament two years later, and he remained an M.P., at least nominally, until his father died (thus elevating him to the earldom). The fact that he did not at this time show much distinction in politics is probably due to his involvement at the same time with military matters, in a world now suddenly more combative.

The war with France started in February 1793, and the same year Lord Paget raised the Staffordshire Volunteers, which became more formally known as the 80th Regiment of Foot. Things changed for him fast from then on. The next year he and his regiment were fighting in Flanders.

Much to his frustration he and the regiment had been left waiting uselessly on Guernsey for the first part of 1794, and it was some relief when at last they joined the Duke of York's army. The war seems at first to have been a fairly leisurely affair, disease and the cold winter being much of the time more of a threat than the French army facing them across the Dutch river. In fact apart from one skirmish and a certain amount of manoeuvring on both sides it cannot be said that Paget gained any experience of war at this stage. He returned to England, with the rest of the army, in 1795, and for the next three years suffered the frustration of being a military officer at home.

It was during this period that he married. He married the daughter of the Earl of Jersey, Lady Caroline Villiers, who was then aged twenty-one. When in due course he rejoined the army it was as Lieutenant-Colonel of the 7th Light Dragoons, and now in charge of a cavalry regiment he seems to have found his true military role. That was in 1797. Two years later the war, after a period of inactivity, started hotting up again.

Paget was thirty-one when he took the 7th Light Dragoons, again under the supreme command of the Duke of York, back to the Netherlands, where once again a rather scrappy campaign against a determined French army resulted in eventual retreat, the signing of a truce, and return to England. Lord Paget had in the meantime been much engaged in the action, and had had the opportunity to show his skill in military tactics.

Still a Member of Parliament, and now a Major-General, Paget, like the bulk of the British army, spent the next eight years at home, half expecting invasion, while the war continued at sea. It was not until the Napoleonic wars moved to the Peninsula, in fact, that ground troops were seriously involved. During those years his lordship amused himself by shooting, and raising a large family. In fact before he went back to war he had fathered eight children.

Napoleon's ambition was undoubtedly to invade Britain itself, but in the end the navy stopped him. It was the Battle of Trafalgar, in 1805, which settled the issue. In 1806 it would have been difficult to imagine that much more was going to happen. Sir Arthur Welleseley, the future Duke of Wellington and victor of Waterloo, was, like Paget, a Member of Parliament. The next year he became Chief Secretary for Ireland, and it seemed almost certain that the rest of his career would be centred on Dublin Castle. Napoleon seemed more a threat now to Austria or Russia than to us.

It was his decision to take the war to Portugal and then Spain that suddenly changed the pace of it. Portugal was a traditional ally and trading partner of the British, and proved at first unwilling to break these ties. This gave Napoleon the excuse to annexe it, and at the same time he put his brother on the throne of Spain. The Spanish rose in revolt, and asked for help from Brtiain. This was something of an extraordinary thing in itself, since Spain had so far been on the French side in the war. It was clear though that the opportunity now occurred to engage our considerable forces, and on terms which it seemed at the time would suit us. The French were having difficulty keeping any sort of grip on Spain and had been restricted to a small area of Portugal. It must have seemed that to defeat Napoleon there would lead to a decisive change in the course of the war.

The first expedition, under Sir Arthur Wellesley, had some success in Portugal, and Paget himself arrived in the troops commanded by Sir John Moore, in north-west Spain. Political vacillation for a time hampered the course of the war, and it was not until Sir John Moore was made commander-in-chief that the matter could begin in earnest. Moreover this decision meant that Paget could at last obtain a position worthy of his rank and ability. He was put in charge of the cavalry.

It was not to be a particularly heroic campaign, however. The Spanish armies they were supposed to be supporting were dispersed and to a large extent already defeated by the French. When Napoleon himself marched against them with fifty thousand men, Moore decided that the only possible course was retreat. He headed for La Coruna, in Galicia, as a port from which he could take his force to the so-far unconquered region of Seville, and aid in its defence. That was the plan, but even that failed to come off.

All the way across the mountains of Galicia in pouring rain, the French army snapping at their heels, broken in spirit and drunk on local wine, the English army presented more the look of a rabble than a disciplined force. It was the function of the cavalry to lead the way, but the ground was hard on the horses' feet, and limping and led by their riders they presented more of an encumbrance than an aid. There was, however, to be one brief interlude of glory.

Learning the whereabouts of a troop of French cavalry Paget detached his horse artillery to confront them. At last he found himself pursuing the pursuers, and he led (as he must often have longed to do) a cavalry charge. The French were triumphantly routed, and for a moment it must have seemed as if the course of things had changed. Napoleon, however, had other ideas.

The break had come because he had deflected a large part of the army to lead an assault on Madrid, which was still maintaining its independence. Madrid capitulated, and he now turned his full attention again to destroying Moore. The latter was expecting this, and all the time prepared to renew his retreat. This he now did in earnest. Paget's job now was to keep up sufficient skirmishes to mask Moore's retreat.

There were to be two more notable events in this phase of the war. The first was a famous, though temporary, victory over Napoleon's cavalry, at Benevente on 29th December, 1808. The sight of the pride of Napoleon's army in flight before the 10th Hussars, with Paget leading, did much to restore the army's low morale.

The next event however took place after Paget himself had left Coruna, although news of it, we are told, came by boat to him at sea. It was Moore's last victory. On 16th January, 1809, he turned and fought, a last desperate and courageous measure to ensure his army's safe retreat. In this he succeeded, since the French were massively defeated. The army embarked in safety; but Moore, mortally wounded in the fray, was not to be with them. His men buried him at Coruna in his cloak, and after they had gone the French erected a monument to an enemy they admired.

At this point it must be said that although the facts of all the foregoing are readily available in standard and specialist histories relating to the subjects and periods, for news of the future Marquess's personal life, both now and throughout this story, we must turn elsewhere. I could not tell this tale, in fact, had it not already been (more expertly) done.

The story of his distinguished ancestor is told by the present (seventh) Marquess in his book 'One-Leg', recently re-issued and highly recommended to all who would know more details of the first Marquess's career. Lord Anglesey had, of course, unique access to source material, particularly Paget's and his family's letters, which he quotes in his book at length. We are thus lucky enough to get a close, behind-the-scenes, view of his great-great-grandfather's private life. He had, we are told, found time in between his Spanish trips to start an affair, which, much to the distress of his wife, he continued after his return. Moreover, such is the small world inhabited by the characters with whom we are currently dealing, it was with the wife of the younger brother of the man who was to become his superior officer, Sir Arthur Wellesley, later Duke of Wellington. We cannot help feeling that perhaps this was a course of action which might have been better avoided, at least in so far as our inevitable sympathy for the unfortunate husband, Henry Wellesley, and Paget's equally unfortunate wife must jar a little with the admiration one naturally feels for a hero of Paget's stature. For present purposes, however, our main concern must be with the effect which this course of behaviour had on his military career.

It is, on the face of it, a puzzle as to why Paget took no further part in the Peninsular War, when he was so well equipped to do so. The war recommenced in April the same year, 1809, with Sir Arthur Wellesley as commander-in-chief of the British army. I think it is clear that Paget could not have served under Wellington in any case, since (as the 7th Marquess points out) he was his senior. In rank they were in fact the same, both becoming Lieutenant-General in 1808; but Paget was almost exactly a year the older. Wellseley's youth and relative inexperience in war (he was still, in the spring of 1809, acting the part of bureaucrat in Dublin Castle) were contentious points. Even the Cabinet, recommending him to the king as leader of the campaign, noted the inconvenience that might arise from 'Sir Arthur Wellesley's being so young a Lieutenant-General', mentioned 'the claims of distinguished officers . . . who are his seniors', and pointed out that it would be open to His Majesty in future, if it seemed best, 'to confide it to a general officer of higher rank'.

Even if this had not been an obstacle to Paget's serving, he could hardly have fought alongside a man, at this particular time, whose family were taking him to court and challenging him to duels. When matters settled down he and Wellesley, who had served together before, became good friends. For the time being however Paget's life was in something of a turmoil; and the 7th Marquess notes his elopement too as a reason why he did not go to Spain.

It was, we must remark, a surprisingly headstrong thing for a supposedly disciplined man to do. Indeed he seems to have found the whole thing rather surprising, perhaps even guilt-inducing, himself. 'It is fought against for a long time', (he wrote to his brother Charles, early in 1809), 'Alas, not long enough – passion gets the better of reason and finally we are driven to the necessity of the present step.' The present step, however, elopement, would seem (in a time when clandestine affairs were carried on quite successfully for years) hardly to be an absolute necessity.

The actual elopement seems in fact to have been her idea, not his, and it followed a row with her husband, Henry Wellesley. The latter had come to suspect her affair with Paget, which was probably an open secret, and on accusing her of it said that one of them must leave; which she did. It was thus not entirely Paget's fault that he was summoned the next day to the support of a lady in distress, in a Hackney coach in Park Lane.

He took her to the house of an army friend, where they spent the night. This gave everybody the chance to calm down, and in any case in the meantime Henry Wellesley had managed to send a letter by one of his wife's servants offering to take her back. The next day she replied to this, via another friend.

This is all rather a long way from the war in Spain. It was that same spring that Sir Arthur Wellesley led the army into the last phase of the Peninsular campaign, while in London his brother and his future second-in-command were competing, with various degrees of dignity, for the former's wife. It was, it seems, the lady who called the shots. When invited to return, she would not go. Her reasons were admirable – she had proved herself unworthy of him; she professes that she resisted 'this most criminal most atrocious attachment'. Yet we must reflect that a little more resistance might have done the trick.

Both her long-suffering husband and Paget's aging father wrote to beg her to give up her wayward affair. Paget's family likewise begged him to go back to his wife. The latter was understandably heartbroken, and Paget's family hastened to try to comfort her. The whole thing had been conducted in such a public style, however, that it was difficult for Paget to get out of it, though it seemed clear to his brothers that he would have liked to. They blamed the woman as temptress, and indeed his lordship's behaviour can only adequately be explained by witchcraft. His brother Charles, in a letter quoted in 'One-Leg', is eloquent on the subject: 'My God, how dreadful, and all this unbounded misery and disgrace and for the most wicked and profligate whore and liar that ever hell itself could or ever will produce.'

His mistress, Lady Wellesley's, brother, Lord Cadogan, now challenged him to a duel, though this was at the time illegal. Paget declined, on the grounds that his responsibility was to devote his life to protecting his mistress, since she had, through their elopement, lost everything.

Wellesley, the aggrieved husband, then instituted legal proceedings, which Paget did not contest. The court awarded damages against him of £20,000, plus costs. Matters now proceeded on Wellesley's side to divorce, but on Paget's they remained complex. He made his mistress an allowance, and went back to his wife. With Charlotte Wellesley now apparently adequately catered for, his previous reason for refusing a duel (that his death would leave her helpless) now apparently no longer applied; when Cadogan challenged him again, in May, he accepted. They met on Wimbledon Common early in the morning of 30th May.

It seems from the report of the seconds (again quoted in full in 'One-Leg') that Cadogan was serious in his intention of destroying Paget, but missed; while Paget, though prepared to take the risk of being killed, had no desire to harm a man whom he recognised he had wronged, and so aimed wide. If this is so it was by chance that we were not, there and then, deprived of a future military and political hero.

He was then, we have to remind ourselves, aged forty-one – too old, we may think, to be behaving in this fashion, and late in the launch of what was to be such a distinguished career. He spent most of his time in London, but visited his estates at Beaudesert and in Devon. We do not hear of him, at this stage, going to Wales. It seems that politicians at home were watching the course of the war and waiting for the best time to launch the remaining army. While Paget was behaving scandalously in London, the army under the elder Wellesley was inching forward towards the enemy in Spain, ill-disciplined and under-supplied, supported by an unpredictable and unprofessional Spanish army.

When the bulk of the army finally entered the war it was again into the Low Countries. Paget (who, it may well be supposed, needed the distraction) was in command of a column of infantry. Although the exercise was inconclusive, and the enemy in this area posed little threat, once again he is lucky to have escaped with his life. A large part of the army was wiped out by fever, spread by mosquitoes from the water-logged ditches in the hot August weather. The French had Antwerp heavily defended, and the remnants of the British force came ingloriously home.

Paget was thus faced again with his marital dilemma. For the time being both the women were nominally back with their husbands (or in

Lady Wellesley's case ex-husband, since the divorce was in the process of becoming finalised in the House of Lords). To add to the bizarreness of all this she was pregnant by Paget at the time, and gave birth to his daughter the next spring. Once the Wellesley divorce was through there was only the obstacle of Paget's wife preventing him from marrying his mistress. Interestingly male adultery was not a ground for divorce in England, so that it was necessary for him to go and commit adultery in Scotland, which he obligingly did. Once this farce had been duly played out both parties were free to marry again, Paget's ex-wife being already, by then, engaged to the Duke of Argyll.

All in all, as he entered middle age, Lord Paget was not in the best of shape. As a soldier he was associated with the most recent disaster, the failed attack on Antwerp, and he now remained unemployed for some years. Socially he had the burden of an unacceptable new wife. It is said that the divorce and settlement had cost him in all some £50,000. Now when his father died in 1812 he found the family businesses to have been so long neglected that, from vast wealth, there was now a real danger of debt. Lord Uxbridge had, simply, been spending more than his lands were earning. This must have taken some doing, but Paget's costly divorce is an example of how it could be achieved.

As peace seemed to be imminent in Europe, with Napoleon's downfall, trouble erupted at home, briefly engaging the attention of Lord Uxbridge, as Henry Paget now was. The so-called Corn Law of 1815 was designed to avoid a collapse of agricultural prices when the artificial circumstances of the war (which kept domestic prices high and encouraged investment in agriculture) suddenly ceased to apply. Britain was now, however, becoming increasingly an urban country, and the industrial proletariat while in no position to benefit from agricultural protection suffered the result of high prices of food. The anti-Corn-Law riots of early 1815 were a symptom of a new division in British social and economic life. The riots grew serious enough to have to be controlled by military power, and Uxbridge was put in charge of this. He thus saw active service for the first time for nearly six years, but in London.

It was by now the second week in March. The Congress of Vienna had been sorting out the future of Europe for almost a year. Napoleon had been holding court on Elba and closely watching developments. At the end of February he decided it was time to leave. On 1st March he landed at Cannes with some eight hundred men and at once began the march to Paris.

This all took the grandees mustered at Vienna by surprise, and by the time the Duke of Wellington (representing Britain at the Congress) had

Uxbridge House, near Savile Row, was the town house of the 1st Marquess's family

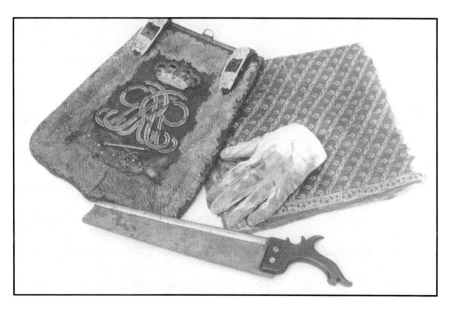

The saw used to amputate Lord Paget's leg, together with a glove and satchel, are now displayed in the military museum at Plas Newydd

gone to Brussels to take charge of the allied forces Napoleon was back in the Tuileries.

The prospect of the war starting all over again was not an appealing one, and the throng gathered in Brussels seems to have hoped that the threat posed by Napoleon would somehow go away of its own accord. People had started to travel abroad again, and there was something of a party atmosphere in Brussels when Wellington arrived. Much of the British army was engaged in North America defending Canada from attempted invasion by the United States. Wellington was in fact in command of an army in which there were more than twice as many foreign troops as British. Because the American expedition had required only infantry, the one thing which he had at his disposal was plentiful cavalry; the important issue therefore was, if there should be a war, who would command this. The success or otherwise of any forthcoming campaign depended on the right choice in this.

It was probably not for personal reasons that Wellington did not want Uxbridge. The unfortunate marital scandal was now thoroughly in the past. The two were bound to meet in social as well as military contexts, and a time of war would have overcome personal considerations. There was now no problem of rank, since Wellington had been promoted to Field Marshal. The fact was that he wanted another officer to command the cavalry, Lord Combermere, with whom he had fought in the Peninsula. Uxbridge was favoured by the Prince Regent, and had the powerful backing of the Duke of York. The fact is that it was a near thing: Lord Uxbridge might quite easily not have been at Waterloo and so not have had his elevation and his subsequent career.

Gradually, in spite of the missing infantry, a considerable army built up along the Belgian border with France, much of it Dutch, under the Prince of Orange, with, in alliance with this but commanded by Marshal Blücher, an army of 89,000 Prussians. In this formidable array Uxbridge's cavalry formed a significant part. At the last minute the Prince of Orange asked him to take command of the Dutch and Belgian cavalry too, and this brought the total of the men for whom he was responsible up to 14,500.

The army gathered at the end of May and waited during the first week of June. The other side of the Belgian frontier the French were gathering. Napoleon himself was now there. By 15th June they were putting the Prussians under pressure, and the following day these received a bad mauling at the battle of Vigny, while Wellington commanded a spirited defence at Quatre Bras. The day ended with Wellington's army retreating in pouring rain to take up a defensive position on a ridge in front of

Waterloo. That night Lord Uxbridge came to consult with the Duke. He asked (according to Philip Guedalla in his book 'The Duke') what was his plan of campaign. The reply was that it depended what Napoleon would do, since Wellington expected him to attack first. 'There is one thing certain, Uxbridge; that is, that whatever happens you and I will do our duty.'

Guedalla says that the Duke then laid his hand on Uxbridge's shoulder, which, if correct, implies reconciliation between them. Uxbridge was, he says, his second-in-command, a fact which is widely known but strangely contradicted by Sir Walter Scott in his life of Napoleon Buonaparte, where he clearly states that General Picton 'at Lord Wellington's special request, had accepted of the situation of second in command'.

Basically Uxbridge was again, as at La Coruna, in charge of covering a retreat. Wellington got the infantry away from Napoleon's advancing cavalry, which was only held back by Uxbridge's horse artillery. It is strange to realise that these great and glorious episodes in our military history were in fact precarious retreats. It seemed to Napoleon that if he could keep Blücher and the Prussians on the run, to which task he despatched Mareschal Grouchy with 32,000 men, then he could safely launch his main army against Wellington, now, by the night of 17th June, successfully retreated to Waterloo.

Although it had stopped raining, on the morning of the 18th, so heavy had been the summer deluges of the days before that what many accounts remember most about the battle is the mud. It was the muddy state of the road which delayed the Prussian army, one corps of which was left to hold off Grouchy, from coming to Wellington's aid. The Duke had to defend himself until they came (late in the afternoon) when he was strong enough to attack. In the meantime Napoleon had suffered from the rain as well, being on the move all that foul night, and arrived at what was to be the field of battle with a wet and hungry army.

It hardly seems like cavalry conditions, but it was in fact Uxbridge's use of both his heavy and light brigades which formed the most notable episodes of the battle.

In fact one of the first events was a charge by the heavy cavalry, which, according to contemporary accounts and to his own later reminiscence, went too far into the enemy's lines, encountering the infantry and on being repulsed suffering severe loss at the hands of the French cavalry. Even so it seems likely that this historic charge, with Uxbridge at its head, was a decisive moment in the course of the famous victory. Uxbridge's job from then on was to lead the remnants of his cavalry in repulsing the successive waves of attack by Napoleon's. In all these actions Uxbridge led from the front, continually putting himself in grave danger, and it is said that while being everywhere that there was action during the hectic central period of the battle, he had eight or nine horses shot from under him. Indeed so careless was he of his own safety during this long day that it is surprising that in the end all he lost was his leg.

Lord Uxbridge lost his leg towards the very end of the action, after Wellington had ordered the final advance, and a cavalry charge, closely followed by the infantry, had the French fleeing in all directions. He was riding alongside the Duke of Wellington, presumably about to join the charge, when a grape shot passed over the neck of the Duke's horse and hit Uxbridge in the right knee, shattering the joint. It was almost the last shot of the battle.

All were agreed that the shattered leg must be amputated, Uxbridge himself taking the whole thing, according to those present, with super-human stoicism. The leg itself was buried by the owner of the house in which the operation happened to take place, in his garden, with a plaque above it which may still be seen. And Lord Uxbridge proceeded to a new (and no less glorious) phase of his career. When, three weeks later, he returned to London fit and well, as if nothing had happened, the Prince Regent, who was a great admirer of his, had already made him a marquess.

The first marquess's father, the first lord Uxbridge of the second creation, had spent much time at his Anglesey property, which perhaps explains why, so far, the first marquess had not. Shortly after inheriting it from his father Sir Nicholas Bayly he had set about redesigning the family seat, Plas Newydd, making it into the graceful, late eighteenth century stately home which it now is, and his improvements continued in the 1790's. That the new marquess took his title from his Welsh property reminds us of the importance of this to his family. The copper mines of Parys Mountain (in which Sir John Wynn had in his time had an interest) had been a valuable source of wealth in the time of Sir Nicholas and the first Lord Uxbridge. When the future first marquess came to Anglesey after the death of his father, however, the mining business had been neglected. His father meanwhile had used his influence and a great deal of money in the control of local politics, and in this the first marquess, now that his military career was over, was to follow him.

The county people of Anglesey were at once eager to honour their Marquess, and fund-raising started only three months after the battle to provide a suitable memorial to the heroic event. A column was agreed on, its location to be within the site of 'the mansion where he occasionally resides' and alongside the main road to Ireland. The column, of grey mar-

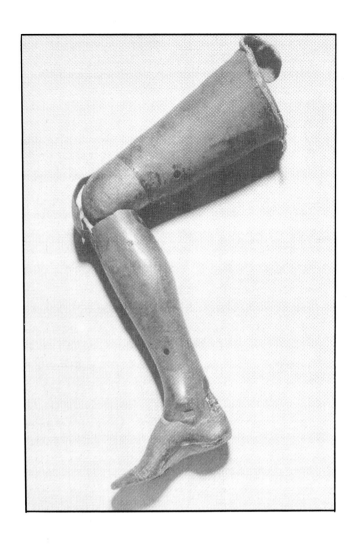

An articulated wooden leg was specially desgined for 'one leg', the 1st Marquess

ble from a quarry at Moelfre, was designed by Thomas Harrison, a prestigious national architect based in Chester. Its construction was started on the first anniversary of the battle, and since it took a year to build its completion conveniently coincided with the second.

It had been traditional for some time for the Paget family to control both the Mayoralty of Caernarfon and the Parliamentary seat of Caernarfon Boroughs, which the first Marquess had held himself as a young man. They dominated the latter, in fact, between the years 1784 and 1830. Lord Anglesey's second son, Lord William Paget, was the Member of Parliament in the 1820's. His brother Sir Charles Paget fought three elections in a row following the change of government, from Tory to Whig, of 1830. Lord Anglesey's influence on the electorate was in the form of sponsorship. It was the custom to provide potential voters with large quantities of food and drink. Presumably the candidate who put up the most lavish feast was expected to win. This exercise in democracy cost Lord Anglesey £1,500 in 1832, and between 1817 and 1821 he had already spent some £5,000 endeavouring to ensure the right outcome to elections. Although this outcome was achieved, not all the money was wisely spent, since a great deal of the hospitality was enjoyed by non-supporters. Professor Dodd comments that on the voting figures, those who voted for Sir Charles in 1832 'must each have consumed on an average, in the course of the eight-day poll, something like twenty dinners and sixteen suppers, seventeen barrels of beer, four gallons of spirit and at least five bottles of wine'. Probably greatly to Lord Anglesey's relief this period of intense involvement in local politics came to an end in 1835, when a Bulkeley Hughes of Plas Coch, a neighbouring and traditionally rival family to the Pagets, defeated the Anglesey candidate. The last Paget stood for Parliament in 1841, and even under conditions of electoral reform this still cost over £1,000.

The Marquess took a less plutocratic interest in the cultural and social life of the area in which he now sometimes lived. It was a time of Welsh cultural revival, a source of pride, as it had been to Sir John Wynn, even to the anglicised local gentry, who were able to feel proud, in the glow of the new fashion, of their ancient roots. When in 1821 the town of Caernarfon held an eisteddfod the Marquess himself was in the chair, although of course his opening speech had to be translated afterwards into Welsh.

That year, 1821, was a busy one for the Marquess. In July he acted as Lord High Steward at the coronation of George IV, his old friend the Prince Regent who had succeeded to the throne the previous year. That August the king sailed to Ireland from the new port of Holyhead, and of

Front and rear views of Plas Newydd, enlarged by the 1st Marquess's father

course he stayed at Plas Newydd in the process.

While the Marquess was thus able to take a renewed interest in his North Wales property, his career in national affairs was by no means over, indeed in many respects it was just starting. In spite of ill-health in the later phases of his life his considerable energy and determination carried him through what were to be virtually two new careers. In 1818 he had been made a Knight of the Garter, and promoted to the rank of full general in 1819. He had to wait then for his first major position. In 1827 he succeeded Wellington in the post of Master-General of the Ordnance. This post (though he was to hold it again) he had for only a few months, before being appointed by Canning, then Prime Minister, to the important position of Lord Lieutenant of Ireland. When Wellington became Prime Minister in January 1828 he found himself once more serving under his old friend and colleague.

Anglesey's job in Ireland was no sinecure. The contentious issue at the time, the 1820's, was the question of catholic emancipation. Theoretically involving catholics all over Britain, the campaign, led by Daniel O'Connell, aimed to free the Irish catholic majority from domination by the Anglo-Irish. O'Connell had been elected to Parliament at a by-election in County Clare, even though as a Roman Catholic he was prohibited from taking his seat. There was, surrounding this issue, a complex web of political conflict, since the king violently opposed emancipation, which put Wellington in a difficult position, as the Duke more realistically saw that war with Ireland was the only alternative to appeasement. Anglesey, in Dublin, was in a harder position still, since he was likely to be attacked by both sides at once. Wellington supported him with arms, but privately hoped that he would hold back from a direct encouragement (which may have seemed the wisest course in Dublin) of the cause of emancipation.

The division in opinion between Wellington and Anglesey was unfortunate for them and for Ireland, but it is explicable if one takes into account that the Prime Minister had to deal more directly with the strong feelings (not to say tendency to bad temper) of the king. It was as much George IV who had Anglesey recalled from Ireland as Wellington. Since the measures which he had advocated (broadly, appeasement to the catholic demands) were then at once put into effect, the assumption at the time was that the Duke wanted to get the praise himself for this breakthrough, and not to let his old competitor have it. The two had taken to corresponding on the subject with other influential figures behind each other's backs, and it was the revelation of this correspondence which made Anglesey's return somewhat scandalous and abrupt.

Whatever its effects on the policies of the Duke and the king, Anglesey's first spell as Viceroy had had such an impact on the mood of the people that it would have been hard for any government to reverse his policy of dealing with the catholic question. The spectacular send-off which the people gave him no doubt sent a message to London. It is clear than an element of competition between the two strong-willed and determined leaders had for a time interrupted their friendship.

Back in London, and idle again, Anglesey was not in the best of health. Ever since the days of his early military career he had been afflicted with a painful form of neuralgia known as 'tic douloureux'. Perhaps this affected him most at times of exhaustion or stress; at any rate he was laid low with it during the first part of 1830, while the king himself was dying at Windsor and the country in some agitation at the prospect of a change of government. Wellington's refusal to countenance Parliamentary reform, which was very much the mood of the people at the time, made his rule so unpopular that it was clear that it was soon coming to an end. The king's death and the consequent dissolution of Parliament, in June, coincided, fortunately, with Anglesey's recovery. It was to prove to be the start of a further phase of his remarkable career.

Lord Grey, the new Prime Minister, knew from the start that he needed Anglesey's help. It was widely recognised that his withdrawal from Ireland had been a mistake, and undertaken for more than political reasons. Grey, with the enthusiastic support of the new king, William IV, at once sent him back to Ireland. But nearly two years had elapsed, and given the protestant establishment a chance to try to undo his creation of goodwill amongst the catholics, thus forcing O'Connell's movement to become more extreme. Lord Anglesey had a good relationship with O'Connell, but the latter's new campaign for nothing less than home rule for Ireland put him in an impossible position. He could see both the sense and the impossibility of it. Ireland was, at the time, too divided to rule itself; and no British parliament would vote for such a course. Such was O'Connell's power over the people that Anglesey now arrived to face a hostile crowd, where just less than two years before he had been so exuberantly fêted.

The confrontation in Dublin between the populist leader and the Viceroy amounted, as Anglesey famously put it, to the question being 'whether he or I shall govern Ireland'. Since he personally had no doubt about the answer, he had O'Connell arrested (for publicly recommending a run on the banks), a dangerous and perhaps rash move under the circumstances. O'Connell himself realised that this might lead to revolt, and opted to pay bail. It was perhaps a fortunate chance that the case never came to court. Events in Ireland were suddenly overshadowed, in the spring of 1831, by the new government's plans for Parliamentary Reform. When O'Connell offered to support this, and for the time being to call a truce in his campaign for Irish home rule, his help was considered so valuable that the case against him was dropped. Indeed the cause of reform occupied most politicians for that year and the next, involving as it did the dissolution of parliament and a general election, in which the government's decision was ratified by its overwhelming return. Anglesey was an avid supporter of reform, and much of his time too was taken in attending the House of Lords to help to steer through the various fiercely-contended bills.

Back in Ireland Anglesey was now involved with another aspect of reform, the old and bitterly felt question of tithes, by which the large catholic majority had to support financially the protestant clergy of the Established Church. In the reform of this manifestly unjust system Anglesey was only partly successful.

His devotion to Ireland and his confidence in his own ability to help it led him to carry on as long as he felt necessary; but we have to remember that he was now aged sixty-five and in constant pain. For one reason or another he felt that by the autumn of 1833 he could safely leave the government of Ireland to others. Largely for the sake of his health (which he thought would be improved in a warmer climate) he headed for Italy, where, sure enough, his painful neuralgia ceased. He had his horses and his yacht sent out, and spent the next year there, in Rome and Naples. Treatment by the founder of homeopathy, Dr Hahnemann, considerably improved his condition (which the sun of Italy had only temporarily relieved); and, rejuvenated by the relief from pain, his social life back to its old form, he was, at this time, only plagued by the misfortunes of his family. His younger son Clarence nearly died of a liver condition (his life saved by the miraculous Hahnemann); and his second son William, (whose profligate life-style and constant threat of disgracing the family by opting for bankruptcy rather than settling his debts, had been a worry and financial drain to his father for some years), caused him so much distress at this time that his complaint returned in earnest. This was the same Lord William Paget who, though much of the time at sea, being an officer in the navy, was also the Member of Parliament for Caernarfon Boroughs. In any case it seems, with hindsight, that it was not so much the homeopathic medicines administered by Dr Hahnemann as the complete though temporary relief from stress brought about by his long period abroad which had led to the diminishing of his attacks. The same effects of simply (as we would now put it) being on holiday applied to the new watering places, which Lord Anglesey also frequented. During these years of leisure, when the only worries were personal, he lived mainly at Beaudesert, where he entertained lavishly.

Now in his seventies, he was becoming noticeably restless at the long period of absence from public life. In 1839 he set off for Russia in his yacht, for instance, ostensibly to foster good relations and avert the war with England which eventually occurred. In spite of a further change of monarch, when Queen Victoria succeeded he remained still a powerful influence at court, where many of his relatives also had positions.

The records of the time mention his excellent horsemanship, remarkable in a man of seventy with a wooden leg; and he himself mentions that Dr Hahnemann, the homeopath, 'appeared quite astonished & pleased at my pedestrian achievements'. These feats of mobility were at least partly attributable to the development of an articulated form of wooden leg, an example of which (worn by him) can be seen in the museum at Plas Newydd. Here too are other remarkable memorabilia, such as the trouser leg which still bears the signs of the mud of Waterloo.

Just when he thought that his old age would be spent yachting in the Menai Strait and the Solent, political confusion surrounding the repeal of the Corn Laws resulted in a change of government in 1846, upon which Lord John Russell, becoming Prime Minister, called on Lord Anglesey to take the post (for the second time) of Master-General of the Ordnance. The next year he was elevated (not before time, we may feel) to the rank of Field Marshal. For the next few years he put into the largely administrative job of Master-General the same energy, conscientiousness and problem-solving ability which he had always displayed in political office. While coping tirelessly with a barrage of dispatches he still found time to entertain at Beaudesert, where he continued to lead the game shooting. It seemed as if this might simply have gone on indefinitely, but he left office as he had come to it with a sudden change of government. When he then finally retired from public life he was nearly eighty-four.

He survived by almost a year and a half his old colleague, and eventually close friend, the Duke. Their lives had been so closely involved right to the end that Anglesey must have felt unbalanced by the loss. He bore his former chief's baton in the cortege at the great state funeral. His isolation was further increased by the death of his wife. He was growing inconveniently deaf. There was not a lot of future to live for, when, in 1854, he had a stroke.

When he died in April 1854, aged nearly eighty-six, the Queen in person demanded a state funeral. She herself, and Prince Albert, and many royal and noble families, attended the procession. The interment however took place not in London but in Lichfield cathedral, where the Pagets had a family vault.

Five years later the people of Anglesey raised the money to add to the column they had built him after Waterloo a large bronze statue. It shows him dressed in the uniform of colonel of the 7th Hussars, and wearing the Order of the Bath and the Waterloo medal. The commission was given to the fashionable sculptor Matthew Noble, and the task of raising the enormous work to the column's top, with an elaborate structure of scaffolding, excited much public attention.

By his two marriages the first Marquess had in all eighteen children and these continued such fecundity to produce seventy-three grandchildren. Many of his descendants have continued his distinguished career, to begin with the younger son Clarence becoming an admiral, and another son George more closely following his father by becoming second-in-command to Lord Cardigan in the Crimea War, hence present at the tragedy of the charge of the Light Brigade.

During his lifetime the first Marquess had often contemplated disposing of some of his properties, and would, if he had had the right offer, have sold Uxbridge House itself. This was now sold, on his death. Today it forms the West End branch of the Royal Bank of Scotland.

Of the other properties, Beaudesert remained within the family until it was put on the market in 1924. It failed to find a buyer, and remained for sale and neglected (having till then been maintained in excellent condition) until it was bought by a firm of housebreakers in 1934. Demolition started at once. Some of the bricks went to the repair of St James's Palace, a building of the same period. The demolition sale was attended by Sir Edward and Lady Hayward, a couple who were building a Tudor-style house in South Australia, as a result of which the grand staircase, panelling and other furnishings of Beaudesert may be seen today in Carrick Hill, at Springfield, a suburb of Adelaide.

Of all their noble properties the one the Angleseys retained was the North Wales one, Plas Newydd, a gracious 18th century house right on the Menai Strait. The Gothic look which the architects James Wyatt and Joseph Potter had given it in 1795 was toned down by the removal of battlements from around the top by the 6th Marquess during the 1930's. Lord Uxbridge had also demonstrated his up-to-date tastes in landscaping by commissioning Humphry Repton (whose innovative style favoured the heightening rather than formalising of the effects of nature) to design the gardens, in 1799. Some of the great beech trees of Repton's layout are still intact. The house contains, besides the Waterloo museum, a truly remarkable mural painted by Rex Whistler for the previous, 6th, marquess, between 1937 and 1940.

The house, grounds and surrounding land now belong to the National Trust, given by the present marquess in 1976. He and the Marchioness still occupy the top floor of the house. The present marquess is a distinguished military historian, whose works, as well as the biography of his ancestor which has been the main support of this chapter, include an eight-volume 'History of the British Cavalry'.

Lloyd George

It is a commonly held fallacy that if you are born in Wales you are Welsh. This would perhaps be technically the case if Wales were an independent Nation State; but since (it hardly needs to be pointed out) it is not yet that, this is not a matter of the right to hold a Welsh passport. Being Welsh is rather more like an ethnic matter, not affected by place of birth, like being a Jew or a Gypsy. The characteristic cannot be acquired, except through some generations of inter-marriage. This is just as well for logical consistency, since Lloyd George was undoubtedly Welsh. And Lloyd George was born in England.

He was born at number 5 New York Place, Robert Street, Chorlton-on-Medlock, on 17th January, 1863. It is an inner suburb of Manchester, lying about half a mile due south of London Road station. The house in question was demolished during the 1950's. In any case the infant David was not there for long.

It was pure chance that he was born there. The Georges had no connection with Manchester. They were a Pembrokeshire family of possibly Flemish origin, if so ironically part of a Flemish colony brought there by Henry II to combat the Welsh. They were comfortable farmers in the Fishguard area. David's father went into the teaching profession, went to London as a tutor, acquired a teaching job at the age of twenty-four which took him to Liverpool, and eventually back in Pembrokeshire became the head of grammar school at Haverfordwest. From there he graduated to another at Pwllheli, where he met, and in due course married Elizabeth Lloyd, then working as a lady's companion in a country house. She came from Llanystumdwy, a small village on the river Dwyfor near Criccieth. They were soon on the move, since he then acquired a teaching post in Newchurch in Lancashire where the first of their children, Mary, was born. From there he took a temporary position in Manchester, which turned out to be his last, since, perhaps already tubercular, he gave up teaching then for reasons of health and retreated with his wife and now two children to take up market gardening on a small farm near Haverfordwest. That was in the early part of 1864. What should have been an idyllic childhood for the one-year-old David was brought to a tragic, but fateful, halt by his father's death from complications after catching a cold, at the age of forty-one, in June of the same year.

We thus have Elizabeth Lloyd a long way from home with two small children and no means of support.

The Lloyds were a family from the Llŷn peninsula who in the early years of that century had set up a shoemaking business in the village of Llanystumdwy, in a workshop alongside the house called Highgate in the main street. Elizabeth's father, Dafydd, after whom no doubt our hero was named, died in early manhood, and his widow Rebecca stalwartly carried on his business. She was assisted in this as soon as he was big enough by her son Richard. The two ran it with some success during the period in which Elizabeth married William George.

In the plight in which she now found herself the widow Elizabeth naturally sent for help to her brother Richard, who (though he had apparently never before left Llanystumdwy) now made the arduous journey down to Pembrokeshire, arranged for the sale of property and settling of affairs, and in due course brought his sister, niece and nephew back with him to live at Highgate. One important detail is that among the chattels which he rescued and brought with them were a large number of books. The school-master had accumulated a library. Both sides of the family were serious-minded Baptists.

It was now the autumn of 1864 and Elizabeth was again pregnant. Richard Lloyd thus found himself, though a bachelor, effectively the foster-father of three children, when the youngest, William, was born in February 1865.

He was then aged thirty. Uncle Lloyd, as the children called him, was a co-pastor and popular preacher at the Baptist church at Cricieth. In the village and the area he was held in high respect. There was, it seems, nothing sanctimonious about this. He was a humble man. The tone with which his younger nephew William writes about him is one of nostalgic affection.

In the Lloyd George Museum near to where he used to live we see in the portrait of him in later life a mild-eyed, heavy-featured man with a long white forked beard. It would not be out of place to pay this some attention. His early teaching moulded the outlook of the future statesman. Throughout his career Lloyd George would seek, and sometimes get unasked, Uncle Lloyd's advice on affairs of state. It is fair in view of this to surmise that even when that advice was no longer available the then Prime Minister would have used as a rule of thumb the question 'What would Uncle Lloyd have done?' 'I cannot over-estimate,' writes his brother William, 'the importance Dafydd attached to Uncle Lloyd's attitude and views upon his activities during those years.' It may have been with a certain desire to please by flattery that he inscribed the copy of the 1910 Finance Act which he presented to him, the outcome of the famous 'People's Budget' of 1909, with the words: 'To Uncle Lloyd, the real author of this Budget, with his pupil's affectionate gratitude, May 31st, 1910.' The gratitude however seems likely to have been sincere. All in all the curious thought remains that the radical and benign principles of this quiet-mannered North Wales shoemaker had a profound effect on British social history.

The village of Llanystumdwy then consisted of about fifty houses. It is still an intimate enough place in an idyllic rustic setting beside the brown, gurgling Dwyfor. 'The river Dwyfor played quite a part in our lives as children,' William George tells us, and indeed this seems inevitable. He and his brother Dafydd (as he always calls him) caught eels there. He says the river does not belong to the village: it is a mere bird of passage of which they had possession for only a few hundred yards. Yet it soon becomes apparent that its passage down the gorge of the Penybont woods and under the old stone bridge forms the essence of the place. In old age Lloyd George took his title from its name, and used to sit and watch it running, on a certain boulder which now lies on his grave. In their childhood, William says, the river kindled in them a sense of the mystery of things.

Ignore the ugly and inappropriate council estate near the turn-off from the main road, and Highgate is almost the first house in the village. It is a semi-detached roadside house in the main street, alongside what is now the Lloyd George museum, a plain, small place, no doubt constricting for the family as the boys grew up.

With a pastor as foster-father the two boys naturally received a religious education. 'I believe Dafydd's overruling passion throughout life was exactly what he said to me during an after-chapel walk in the days of our youth, which was to become a social reformer.' William makes it clear that he means by this an attempt to make civil laws more compatible with divine justice, and he sees this primarily religious quest as lying behind such great practical achievements as the 1910 Finance Act.

It was not a hard upbringing. The Lloyds were essentially middle class, the owners of a small business. The elder sister, Mary Ellen, went to a private boarding school in Cricieth. It was, on the other hand, a simple and basically Welsh existence. Most of the people of Llanystumdwy were

Llanystumdwy, Lloyd Geroge's boyhood home, is a small village on the river Dwyfor

*Lloyd George was brought up in the home of his uncle Richard Lloyd, 'Highgate',
a terraced cottage in the main street*

engaged in agriculture. Perhaps the most significant aspect of life there, in the light of events which it was to influence, was the pattern of land ownership. The greater part of the parish was owned by the local squire, Hugh Ellis Nanney. The remainder was in the hands of three spinsters who lived in Trefan Hall above the village. These were remote figures and played little part in village life. This on its own seems unlikely to have inspired a radical outlook, since although it may have seemed unfair that land should be owned by one person and worked by many, this was (and indeed still is) the normal pattern in rural areas.

It was the chapel outlook, surely, the religious and not the social circumstances of his childhood, which made Lloyd George take the attitude he did.

Since he was in Llanystumdwy from the age of two to that of seventeen we can hardly ignore the effect which village life might have had. The boys took a full part in chapel life and in the Liberal politics which went with it. At the age of five David carried a banner in an election campaign, though he can hardly have been aware of the reason. He made his first speech in a chapel competition at the age of fourteen. Although he had little contact with the world beyond Criccieth he followed the national news from the age of eleven. He was, by some accounts, a spoilt child, and precocious. He read and memorised his uncle's books. He had been at school from the age of three years seven months, and although as a Church school the education had an English bias his first language was Welsh. The family were Baptists, and it was at the Baptist church of Penymaes at Criccieth, in fact in the stream behind it, that his Uncle Lloyd baptised him, in 1875. By the age of eighteen he was preaching himself, in a temporary appointment at Penmachno. As his attention turned increasingly to a career in law, however, his interest in organised religion lessened. He remained throughout his life an attender of Baptist services, but from an early age it became clear that he was not to follow in his uncle's footsteps.

Davy Lloyd, as he was known, had established in the village life of his contemporaries something of a reputation as a leader. He displayed a certain amount of unscrupulousness and ruthless determination. That he was not like the other village boys is sufficiently shown by the determination with which he then set about fulfilling his ambition. He studied conscientiously for the law, took and passed the Law Society exam at Liverpool at the age of fourteen, and the next year, aged fifteen, went to work with the firm of Breese, Jones & Casson, solicitors in Porthmadog, where, for the time being, he lived in a boarding house.

In the spring of 1880 the family moved from Llanystumdwy to a rented house in Cricieth. After the death (in 1868) of his mother, on whose business acumen the shoemaking enterprise seems to have relied, Uncle Lloyd had found it increasingly hard to keep up his occupation and eventually had to give it up completely due to ill health. It is this time which William George cites as being the period of real poverty in their early lives, and it is indeed difficult to see what they lived on. The two brothers were now both articled clerks, and relied on gifts rather than wages from the principle of their firm. Tourism was already the main industry in Cricieth, and to stay alive it was necessary for them to take in paying guests. These introduced a contact with the wider world which no doubt benefited the young boys. One of their paying guests was the novelist H. Rider Haggard, who was probably at the time working on 'King Solomon's Mines' (published in 1886). The elegant, slightly prim terrace where the Lloyds lived is everything a Victorian seaside terrace should be, truly minor bed-and-breakfast stuff, sedate, though quite small and modest.

It is interesting, in view of the end of this story, that the young Lloyd George had left Llanystumdwy without regret. He wrote in his diary on May 9th 1880: 'Slept there for the last time – perhaps – for ever' – an ironic error in prophecy which nevertheless reveals his distaste for the place at the time, expressed more forcefully on May 10th: 'Left Llanystumdwy without a feeling of regret, remorse or longing.' He had of course by then had a taste of small-town as opposed to village life, in Porthmadog, and Cricieth no doubt offered a further expansion of company. Clearly a village would be too enclosing for someone of his mental alertness and social facility. In any case his life was about to branch out.

To take the Law Society Intermediate exam he had to go to London. Uncle Lloyd's co-pastor at Penymaes gave him 40/- towards the expense of the journey. He wrote immediately on his arrival, the first of many such letters home. While in London he did some sightseeing, including a visit to the House of Commons. He found it disappointing – 'inside they are crabbed, small and suffocating' – and his diary note makes it clear that he already had an aspiration of one day ruling there: as he puts it, he saw himself as eyeing the Assembly in the spirit with which William the Conqueror viewed England when he visited Edward the Confessor. ' . . . as the region of his future domain. Oh! Vanity.'

He was back in London in the spring of 1884 for his Finals, and watched a debate in the House of Commons. An interest in politics had been growing in him in this time. He had helped as a party worker in the 1880 election. In 1882 participation in the Porthmadog debating society had given him a chance to practise speaking. From 1880 he had also begun to express himself through journalism. He was much impressed by hearing Joseph Chamberlain speak at Denbigh, in 1884. Chamberlain was then President of the Board of Trade in the Liberal Government of William Gladstone, a post Lloyd George himself was to hold in due course with notable success. Chamberlain held strong views on the issue of Irish Home Rule, eventually resigning from the government on the production of a Home Rule bill, which he opposed. Again Lloyd George was not to know at the time that he himself would one day have to deal with this problem.

The same year the Franchise Act had the effect of more than doubling the Welsh electorate, thus putting an end to the power of the gentry over votes. This not only favoured the Liberals in Wales, against the more anglicised Conservatives; it also favoured the cause of Welsh religious disestablishment, the anglicised gentry being firmly associated with the Church of England, which still held control of religious funding.

The 1886 Merioneth by-election took place in this new political landscape, and for a time it seemed as if Lloyd George would be the candidate. In the event he withdrew his name, ostensibly in favour of his friend and Liberal colleague Tom Ellis, who then got in. In his diary he makes it clear that he was not yet ready, chiefly because he thought he could not yet afford the lifestyle. The campaign gave him the chance of a speaking tour of south Caernarfonshire, in which he attacked the tithe system which lay at the core of the fight for disestablishment.

In the meantime he had been trying to build up a legal practice of his own. At the end of the year in which he qualified, 1884, he left the Porthmadog firm and set up his own business in the family home at Cricieth. This was, in William's account, a hard time. He himself qualified as a solicitor and joined his brother in practice in 1887. Never adopting the second name, the 'Lloyd' being David's personal trademark, he continued in practice himself and later with his son, under the title 'William George & Son', a firm which still exists in Porthmadog High Street. His timing in joining his brother was, for him, unfortunate. In December the next year David was adopted as Parliamentary candidate for Caernarvon Boroughs, and a good deal of his time from then until his election to Parliament was spent fostering his candidacy. William did not realise how soon the job of building up the practice would devolve on him. 'Still less,' he says with mild bitterness, 'did I realize how soon it would be my privilege to be, in the main, the bread-winner for two families.'

This is because at the start of that same year, 1888, David had got married. The courtship had been going on for some time, but at first in secret. It was not of course his first romance. David was, his brother says,

Mynydd Ednyfed, the farmhouse home of his in-laws, stands prominently above Cricieth

The couple were married in the Methodist chapel at Pencaenewydd

'endowed with qualities which were particularly attractive to women . . .' He never seemed to be content unless he was having an affair. Not just for these reasons, but because of his reputation for outspoken views and his relative poverty and lack of prospects, he would not have been at all the choice of the household at Mynydd Ednyfed, on whose heiress he had set his sights.

Mynydd Ednyfed is a substantial old farmhouse which still wears an air of status, standing proudly up on its hill right above Cricieth town. It looks as if it is looking down on you, and it must have taken courage for the young solicitor to think that he could ascend that hill and breach its defences. The Owen family were prosperous farmers, approaching the level of gentry. Richard Owen was a leading deacon at the Calvinistic Methodist church. It takes some knowledge of the strangely factional world of Welsh Non-Conformism to realise that this did not mean they would welcome a Baptist into the family. For all these reasons the courtship took place in secrecy for some three years.

Possibly the prospect of a Parliamentary career rather than that of a small-town solicitor changed the balance; for some reason, at any rate, the affair became more open after 1887. Early in 1888 they were to be married. There remained the temporarily insuperable problem of agreeing the denomination of the chapel in which this could take place.

Margaret Owen emerges into this story and runs right through it as a figure of some integrity, who, from a sheltered background, had no chance of anticipating what life with Lloyd George would be like. William quite clearly liked and admired her, though he, like everybody else who writes about her, has some difficulty avoiding a tone of pity. To pity her by itself would be too patronising. She was a strong woman with a strong sense of principle and a firm understanding of her role. She was also a human being and consequently had the capacity to be hurt.

William put his finger on one aspect of her personality which was to become almost at once a problem. In common with him she preferred the country to the town. David on the other hand, in spite of his rural upbringing, gained a stimulus from the bustle of urban life. It was perhaps foolish of Margaret not to foresee this conflict. She knew quite well when they married that he had political ambitions which he was actively pursuing and at the time working to gain a candidacy. Perhaps she thought this would come to nothing, but it is unlikely that anyone would so have underestimated him. Perhaps she foresaw the life of the wife of a constituency M.P. Perhaps love for him at the time simply obliterated any such sort of assessment. At any rate though throughout their marriage she did her duty as ministerial consort, it is noticeable that whenever she could, and for longer and longer periods, she came home to Cricieth.

The Owens wanted a quiet ceremony in a Methodist chapel. David favoured a Baptist one in the country outside Cricieth. In the end both parties agreed to a compromise whereby the Methodist chapel at Pencaenewydd, a tiny village in the hinterland of Cricieth, acted as neutral territory, presumably as the place of worship of neither party. It must come as something of a shock to this self-effacing place, with its squat little plain grey chapel squeezed between houses in its main street, to find itself mentioned in history.

The marriage took place on 24th January, 1888 before a handful of relatives. David came by train from Cricieth to Chwilog with Uncle Lloyd, from where they walked. They drove in a closed carriage back to Chwilog, from where the newly-weds took a train to Euston for a ten day honeymoon.

Against all probability the Owens seem to have taken to their new son-in-law. The young couple went to live with them at Mynydd Ednyfed. That was it would seem where he was when he started his new career. At the same time the family began to grow, Richard being born on 15th February 1889, and Mair Eluned 2nd August 1890. The Owens, retiring from farming, built two semi-detached houses on the Porthmadog road in Cricieth, one for themselves and one for their daughter's family. These (next to the Bodlondeb hotel) are very fine, substantial buildings, indeed verging on the magnificent. By then the latter also had lodgings in London, in Grays Inn Road.

The constituency of Caernarvon Boroughs, as it was then called, consisted of the town of Caernarfon itself and the other of Edward I's chartered boroughs in the area, Pwllheli, Nefyn, Cricieth, Conwy and Bangor. It was a seat traditionally held by the Conservatives. The death of the sitting M.P. led to a by-election in April 1890, a year and a quarter after David had been chosen as Liberal candidate and three months after his twenty-seventh birthday. It is significant and ironic that the Tory candidate against whom he had to contend was the landowner of the Llanystumdwy area, Hugh Ellis Nanney. Lloyd George campaigned on the issues of Irish home rule, Welsh disestablishment, land reform and justice for farm workers, decentralisation of government, universal franchise, graduated taxation, and, another Non-Conformist principle which was always dear to him, temperance. In view of some of the effects of his time in power we shall have reason to applaud him for consistency.

It was a nail-biting finish, and one of those occasions when a very slight change of circumstances might have had an equivalently great effect on British history. At the first count the Conservatives had a majority. A recount gave Lloyd George a majority of eighteen.

That was the first of fourteen electoral victories stretching over a period of more than fifty-four years. Throughout that period he continued to be the member for Caernarvon Boroughs. He only relinquished his seat in fact, undefeated, when he was elevated to an earldom two months before he died.

When he made his maiden speech Margaret was at home, pregnant with their second child. She joined him in their rooms near the Inns of Court the following year. The speech, in June 1890, was a witty and colourful matter on a minor Liberal amendment to a bill compensating publicans for abolished licences. His second speech had the distinction of giving rise to a complaint from Queen Victoria. It was an attack on the costs of royal pageantry. All his early speeches quickly gave rise to a reputation for entertainment. Temperance was a common theme in them.

Lloyd George had Welsh contacts in London, and attended a Baptist church near Oxford Circus. In Parliament he promoted a bill to give Wales local control over the sale of liquor. He supported Parnell's cause in the question of Irish home rule, though this was to be a losing contest.

Back home brother William kept the business going. David acted as the London agent, and in due course opened another firm in London. He then spent his mornings employed in law, his afternoons and evenings involved in politics. His energy and capacity for work are impressive throughout his career.

He was a short man, only five-and-a-half feet tall. Though broadly built, with a large head, black hair and moustache, he was said to be not physically impressive. It was when he talked that the magic occurred.

One of the issues on which Lloyd George fought the next election was the inadequate plan for old age pensions. This time he won with over fifty-two percent of the vote. This was in July in 1892. Gladstone's government was safely back in power, with no less than thirty-one M.P.'s in Wales, as against only three Conservatives. This gave Lloyd George a powerful argument for urging the party to put Welsh devolution on their agenda. One of the matters troubling Wales was the security of tenure of tenant farmers. Gladstone himself announced that he was appointing a Royal Commission to report on the land question in Wales, thus recognising that it differed from the situation in England. Mr Gladstone, with characteristic flair for theatrical effect, made this announcement from a rock on the slopes of Snowdon, where he had come to open the Watkin footpath. William George and his mother were in the crowd on this occasion, and David of course with the Grand Old Man. He was amongst those invited to have lunch with him by his host, Sir Edward Watkin, and

Lloyd George and his first wife Margaret

reported to his brother that Gladstone did all the talking. There was an age difference of fifty-four years between them, Gladstone then being eighty-three.

Part of the Welsh programme, along with land reform, was the question of disestablishment. The problem here was that the majority of people in Wales belonged to churches other than the Church of England, yet by law contributed to the livings of the Church of England clergy. Recognising an equivalent situation in Ireland, where the majority were Catholic, Gladstone had steered through an Irish disestablishment act in 1869. In Wales however the matter was long delayed, and a bill which might have passed was disrupted by the government's resignation. This failure gave Lloyd George a continuing platform, and he was re-elected in the subsequent general election with a similar majority.

When his mother died in 1896 links with Cricieth became weakened as his activities in London became more intense. For one thing, with his law practice, parliamentary duties and a good deal of public speaking he worked enormously long working days. One wonders when he found the time for his legendary love-life. He also had a full leisure life, being sociable and open in his friendships. As one of his biographers puts it: 'His favourite recreations – other than sex – were reading, choral singing, walking, fishing, and (after about 1895) golf.' All this is evidence of his phenomenal energy.

Margaret's retreat for long periods to Cricieth at this time can be interpreted as either a result or a cause of his philandering. It might have been a sign of her distaste and disappointment, or it might have presented him with both the need and the opportunity to be unfaithful. We have to remember that she now had four children to look after, so may have been reasonably content to carry on her own life in the country. As well as Richard and Mair, Olwen had been born in 1892 and Gwilym in 1894. A fifth, Megan, came along in 1902.

Historians are divided on the question of how much Margaret knew. In the correspondence we find the occasional clue to tension between them: 'You threaten me with a public scandal,' she wrote from Cricieth in August, 1897. However innocent, she could hardly have been fully unaware of his indiscretions, since the matter was an open secret and the subject of gibes in the gossip columns of the time. He was nicknamed the Welsh goat, a supposedly lascivious creature. Perhaps she found it easier to turn a wilfully blind eye from the seclusion of North Wales. This must have been sometimes a hard feat for her, and none more than when Lloyd George was cited in a divorce case, in 1896-7. He himself was away in South America when rumours started to circulate. It concerned a Dr

Edwards of Montgomeryshire, whose wife signed a statement in divorce proceedings citing Lloyd George. Dr Edwards did not believe her, and she eventually withdrew the statement. In court Lloyd George was completely exonerated. The case was however to re-occur many years later, by which time he had reached high office. It seems likely that what actually happened is that the wife used his name as a cover for the real culprit, the credibility of doing so being that Lloyd George had been in the habit of staying with the Edwardses when on speaking tours in Montgomeryshire.

Whether or not Lloyd George loved his wife there is no doubt that she loved him, having married him against her parents' wishes at a time when he had no obvious prospects. Their relationship was to be severely tested at later times, but for the time being it was possible to sustain a modus vivendi.

He travelled a lot, for the time. The visit to South America was followed by a trip to Italy, in 1897, to North Africa the year after and Canada the year after that. Normal life was temporarily interrupted then by the outbreak of the Boer War, in October 1899, which shot Lloyd George to national prominence.

Although not strictly speaking a pacifist, and to some extent in favour of imperialist rule, Lloyd George opposed the war. He was pro-Boer, and in the circumstances this was tantamount to treason. Most of the nation resorted to a hysterical Jingoism (as such popular chauvinism was known, after the chorus of a music-hall song of the 1870's), and only a few people of principle, led as it turned out by Lloyd George, promoted the pro-Boer platform.

The issue was basically a question of the ownership of the South African goldfields in the Transvaal, discovered in 1886, which had transformed the Boers from backward farmers into a potentially threatening power in Africa. Up till then the British had been content to let them occupy the Transvaal in peace. To make the matter more ambivalent, however, the Boers had made the first aggressive move. At the outbreak of the war (the second Boer War, and so familiar territory at the time) they had invaded British South African territory, so that the war started as an attempt to drive them back. 'In my opinion,' wrote Lloyd George in a letter to William, five days after the war had started, 'the way these poor hunted burghers have been driven in self-defence to forestall us, aggravates our crime.' The crime, as he saw it, was the attempt to re-occupy the territory, basically the Transvaal, which had been granted to the Boer republic. Clearly the mass of the population, the government, and particularly Joseph Chamberlain, then colonial secretary, saw the matter differently.

One thing that comes out of this period of his career with striking force is Lloyd George's considerable physical courage. Ten thousand people tried to break into a meeting he held in Glasgow. 'For twenty minutes I stood facing a shouting, yelping, fighting crowd.' He then (according to his own report) silenced them with a couple of sentences. 'A hush instantly fell on the whole audience' and 'I spoke for forty minutes, and got a splendid hearing.' Nevertheless his carriage was attacked as the speakers drove from the meeting, its glass smashed and somebody cut. Lloyd George was uninjured, and continued his speaking tour against the war in spite of being fearful of the result of losing his seat. 'We are fighting for free speech and equal rights in the Transvaal.' At a meeting held at Penrhyn Hall in Bangor, on 11th April 1900, he was physically assaulted by his own constituents. In spite of a strong police escort a vast crowd surrounded the building, and the shouts outside rendered the speakers inaudible. The crowd then began to pelt the roof with stones, succeeding in disrupting the meeting. Lloyd George escaped into a friend's house and out through the back. In spite of this experience he then continued his campaign by addressing a meeting in Nefyn, previously loyal to him but now enemy territory. Here he won over the crowd by describing to them conditions in the notorious British concentration camps in South Africa. This was a matter more fully disclosed to the nation in a letter to The Times from Burdett Coutts in June.

In September Parliament was dissolved. It was, it was clear, to be a 'khaki' election, Joseph Chamberlain in particular intending to use the spirit engendered by the war to boost the party's following. His party, however, was split on the issue, and Lloyd George made it as much an anti-war election. He himself managed to get returned with a majority of 296. When Parliament reassembled in December he made a speech implicitly attacking Chamberlain. The theme was that members should be obliged to declare their interests, the underlying point being that Chamberlain's family (though by now not he himself) were behind the firm of Kynoch's, in Birmingham, and so benefitted from the sale of munitions. The motion was defeated.

Under the circumstances it was surprising that the Birmingham Liberals should have invited him to address them, and in anyone else it would be more surprising that this invitation should be accepted. Birmingham was not only the headquarters of the Chamberlain camp but was doing rather nicely out of the war. Nevertheless he went, on December 18th 1900, amid a hate campaign by the Tories and mob stirring possibly with the connivance of the Chamberlain group, specifically

The Owens, his in laws, built semi-detached houses on the Porthmadog road in Cricieth for themselves and their son-in-law

The death of his daughter Mair Eluned was a severe blow to Lloyd George. The memorial at the family vault is by Goscombe John

aimed at inflicting on him personal injury. He was warned by the police to stay away. Thousands besieged the Town Hall, where he was to speak, screaming 'Traitor! Bloody Traitor! Kill the bloody traitor!' Incredibly Lloyd George, unrecognised, mingled with the crowd before the meeting. The whole city around him was in chaos.

He had no hope this time that he would be able to deliver his speech. He dictated it to a typist for later publication. When he appeared on the platform the crowd got out of control, the mob having forced its way into the Town Hall. The police hurried him off the stage, and he left, famously, disguised as a policeman. The helmet he wore is on view in a glass case in the Museum at Llanystumdwy.

The fame which the war brought him had its disadvantages. His wife and family suffered, as did his business and, William notes, his brother's. His son Dick had to be withdrawn from the school he went to and taken to live with his uncle William at Garthcelyn, in Cricieth, from where he went to the Porthmadog Grammar School. The George family were the only pro-Boers in Cricieth, and in the hysterical chauvinism which greeted the relief of Mafeking (where a British garrison under Baden-Powell had been under siege for seven months) effigies not only of David but of William and Uncle Lloyd as well were burnt on a bonfire. 'That,' says William, 'is the nearest approach I ever made to the crown of martyrdom, and I must say I rather enjoyed the experience . . . ' Nobody, of course, could exonerate the inclusion in this sorry spectacle of Uncle Lloyd.

After the war Lloyd George found himself to be the natural spokesman for liberal Non-Conformism on such matters as education and free trade. On the latter issue Winston Churchill became an ally, and (formerly a Conservative) became a Liberal, in May 1904. He came to Caernarfon to speak alongside Lloyd George. It is interesting to see that Lloyd George's attitudes at this time were largely middle class. He distrusted strikes, favouring adjustment, and took a moderate view of trade unions in general. He opposed the formation of the Labour Party, largely in protection of the Liberals. His Non-Conformist inclination towards temperance, even prohibition (though he was not a teetotaller himself) was hardly likely, at this time, to appeal to the working class. The King, Edward VII, was an admirer. He went so far as to arrange a meeting, getting himself and the young M.P. invited to dinner at Lord Tweedmouth's. For once it seems Lloyd George lost his conversational sparkle. The King asked him if he played bridge. He said he did not. The King said 'That's a pity.' That was the limit of their discussion.

To earn money at this time, since remarkably ordinary M.P.'s were not paid, and therefore had to be part-time politicians, Lloyd George developed a career as a professional speaker, showing lantern-slide shows of his travels. In 1905 a haemorrhage after tonsillectomy obliged him to take a two month holiday by the sea in Italy with his brother William. It was about this time that the Balfour government fell and the Liberals swept to victory with Campbell-Bannerman as Prime Minister. He was quick to promote the already famous young Welshman, who now found himself (with an income of £2000 per year) President of the Board of Trade.

Right from the start he demonstrated a novel approach to running a department. He was, it seems, unable or unwilling to delegate. Shocking and alienating his civil servants he insisted on knowing all about his department himself. Measures which he introduced were usually radical and sometimes rash. An example is the raising of the permitted load line for shipping, the 'Plimsoll Line', with the aim of favouring British freight against competitors. It led to the unfortunate result of the loss of several old and unsafe ships.

He was at the Board of Trade still when his eldest daughter died. Mair Eluned was a talented girl of seventeen. The blow to Lloyd George was severe, and the event probably increased his isolation. He came to Cricieth for the funeral, where Mair was buried first alongside and later within the family vault. In due course a monument designed, like the statue of Lloyd George in Caernarfon square, by Sir Goscombe John, was erected there.

Lloyd George at this time was a hard-working but somewhat solitary figure. He lived alone in Chelsea, from where he walked the two miles to Westminster each morning, and back each evening. He read late into the night. In Government his introduction of a Licensing Bill in 1908 which aimed to reduce the number of pubs by one third over a period of fourteen years was probably the cause of the loss of a seat to the Liberals at the Peckham by-election that spring. His attack on the House of Lords lost him favour with the King. None of this however hindered the upward surge of his career.

In the spring of 1908 Sir Henry Campbell-Bannerman retired as Prime Minister through ill health. Asquith was at the time Chancellor of the Exchequer, and in the course of preparing a bill introducing old age pensions. He was Campbell-Bannerman's natural successor, and the only question that remained was who was to take over the Treasury. Then, as ever, there was the danger of the Liberal party splitting itself in two; C-B had managed to hold the two sides together, the New Liberals with radical reforming ideals, like Lloyd George, and the Gladstonian traditionalists – like Asquith. Lloyd George now made it clear that he would not serve in Asquith's government if someone else was appointed

Chancellor. He did not rule out Asquith remaining Chancellor himself, as Prime Ministers have occasionally done. Asquith, having decided against this latter course, had little option but to appoint Lloyd George. To have the recognised radical leader on the back benches would have amounted to cleaving the party down the vulnerable fissure between its two aspects, which was of course what was in due course to take place.

It was thus, perhaps by chance, perhaps with a sense of opportunism which often seems to have inspired his actions, that Lloyd George came to be the Chancellor of the Exchequer who introduced the Old Age Pension Bill of 1908. He had not (John Grigg points out) even been on the cabinet committee which, with Asquith, framed the bill. No doubt pensions were a subject dear to his heart, but he had not involved himself hitherto in the legislation. Now, suddenly, it was his bill. When people over seventy drew their pensions in the January of the next year they actually talked of going to 'draw my Lloyd George'.

To carry out his ambition of a total package of welfare reform he had to involve himself in the whole matter of taxation. First it would be necessary to reduce the defence bill, which amounted to slowing down the Anglo-German arms race. He understood this better than he understood the sums involved. Lloyd George's lack of education, commented on by those around him, makes his achievement in scrambling to the top of a haughty establishment all the more amazing. The decidedly patrician Asquith remarked to Lord Rendel that he thought Lloyd George 'could neither read nor write'. Margot Asquith referred to him as 'that wretched little lawyer'. It was said of him that as Chancellor 'he never looked at a figure and could not be made to do so.' To Austen Chamberlain he 'made a hash' of the routine functions of his office. Nevertheless he saw quite clearly that heavy naval spending remained a problem for his programme of social reform.

His response to this was to go in for diplomacy. He set about an exercise in what we would now call 'networking' around Europe. First he went to Berlin. The main outcome of this was a Bavarian shepherd's cloak, which he often later liked to be photographed wearing. He called at the fashionable resorts of Carlsbad and Marienbad on his return. At the former he met Clemenceau, the powerful Premier of France. The latter however said to Edward VII at Marienbad a few days later that he was amazed 'by the crass ignorance Lloyd George displayed concerning foreign policy.' These pre-war visits to Germany must remind us, with hindsight, of his visits to Hitler before the second World War, and his bluff approach to international diplomacy now may be at least partly the fruit of naïvety.

It took some time both to draw up and then to revise the famous 1909 budget. The theme was land reform, by means of a capital gains tax on increases in land value. The effect of this, as it turned out, would be to curtail house building and hence raise prices. There was one striking innovation in this: the use of taxation itself to carry out political policy. The budget was intended to be redistributory of wealth. It had a secondary, implicit aim: to provoke the House of Lords into opposing it, and so make the matter of their lordships' power an issue. Apart from land taxes there was to be a higher and more steeply graduated income tax, heavy rates on 'unearned' income, a supertax, inheritance tax (which had existed for some time) was increased by a third, there was a sharp rise in tax on liquor licences and on hard liquor, and also, in a strikingly familiar note, on cars and on petrol.

So modern, and indeed so socialist, is this, that it is hardly surprising that throughout the summer of 1909 it was bitterly contested. When it was first announced, however, on 29th April, the reponse was mainly bafflement. Inexplicably, for someone already famed for his oratory, Lloyd George made a bad speech. Nobody could understand what he was talking about, largely, it was felt, because he didn't understand it himself. The clauses were drafted by his private secretary, and it seems he hadn't read it through beforehand. After three hours, such was the state he was in, Mr Balfour, the leader of the opposition, proposed a half-hour's adjournment, during which the Chancellor collected himself somewhat and made a better job of the remainder.

So great was the controversy surrounding the Budget that Parliamentary recess was cancelled that year, and the debate raged uninterrupted. Lloyd George himself exacerbated this by his famous Limehouse speech on 30th July, in which a latent hatred of the gentry and the landowning classes (perhaps a residue of his childhood at Llanystumdwy) was revealed as the underside of the high principles of social reform. Harcourt remarked to Asquith, of this phase of populist tub-thumping, 'I found all over the country that all Lloyd George's speeches . . . had done us much harm.' The debate continued until October. When the Lords rejected the bill Parliament was dissolved, and a mandate sought by a general election in January 1910, with the additional theme now of parliamentary reform, meaning the removal of the power of veto of the House of Lords.

The harm Harcourt referred to, in connection with that election, was possibly partly responsible for the regaining by the Tories of lost votes, and the new Liberal government found itself reliant on the support of Labour M.P.'s together with that of Irish Nationalists, which in turn led to the need for a new home rule bill. In the meantime Lloyd George suffered the threat of the revival of the divorce scandal which he might well have thought to be a thing of the past, when two newspapers decided, presumably for political motives, to reprint the allegations which had been quashed when he was a backbench M.P., now of more public interest in relation to the Chancellor of the Exchequer. ' . . . is a juicy scandal about a public man ever buried without hope of resurrection?', his brother muses.

The editor of 'The Bystander' apologised at once, blaming a mistake by inexperienced staff, published an apology and offered £300, which Lloyd George accepted and donated to the Caernarfon cottage hospital. The editor of 'The People' was less circumspect, and in March 1909 the matter went to trial. Since the matter had already been thoroughly cleared up by the earlier court hearing Lloyd George probably had no need of his formidable legal team, consisting of Rufus Isaacs, F.E. Smith and Raymond Asquith (the Prime Minister's son). For the defence Sir Edward Carson, a former solicitor general and now an Irish Unionist M.P. (who had made his name as an advocate by his successful defence of the Marquess of Queensbury against Oscar Wilde's suit for libel) now, belatedly recognising the legal standing of his client's case, offered no defence. His client admitted libel and apologised, and Lloyd George accepted compensation of £1000. This he donated to the building of Llanystumdwy's village institute, the plain and serviceable hall which still stands alongside the Lloyd George museum there, a short distance from his grave.

It was at this time (in 1910) that Bryn Awelon was built, a handsome house in a comfortable suburban mock-Tudor style on its own on a hill at the end of a terrace in upper Cricieth, overlooking the bay. It is now a nursing home, sheltered by trees which have grown large around it. He had perhaps the thought of spending more time there, though this was not to be. As it was he spent some weeks there during the recesses, now with a keen interest in playing golf. It was, writes one witness, 'quite an ordinary spectacle,' on the Cricieth links, 'to see the Chancellor, with the village draper as his partner, playing against the village cobbler and Winston Churchill.' His wife Margaret still acted as hostess at No.11, but increasingly now retreated to Bryn Awelon.

In July 1912 the family came to Bryn Awelon with friends for the long recess, this time bringing with them ten-year-old Megan's French and music tutor. Lloyd George was reported to be in exuberant mood this time; there were picnics, games and singing. Bryn Awelon was always full of guests. Frances Stevenson's first appearance in the entourage car-

Llanystumdwy's village hall was built with the libel money Lloyd George received from 'The People'

Bryn Awelon, in upper Cricieth, was built for the Lloyd Georges in 1910

ried nothing ominous about it.

That happy summer in Cricieth however lay in the context of generally gathering clouds. There had been signs of conflict with Germany since the late summer of the year before. That year, besides having the hottest weather on record, when temperatures remained in the 90's for much of early August, saw not only the 'Agadir crisis', in which Britain supported France against Germany in the event of an apparent German attempt to invade Morocco, but also saw Lloyd George's popularity drop with the onset of strikes and great trouble gaining acceptance of his National Insurance bill. He had a throat problem aggravated by tireless speaking, and for a time convalesced, his place in cabinet being taken by Winston Churchill. That year, however, as something of a distraction, he persuaded Parliament and the king to include in the Civil List a large sum for the public investiture of the Prince of Wales at Caernarfon castle, the future Edward VIII being then, in 1911, seventeen. This raised Lloyd George's public image considerably, being so visibly part of royal pageantry. It was that July of 1912, however, that the first results of what was perhaps his biggest innovation became reality, when people actually had to start paying their national insurance contributions.

It is difficult for us now to appreciate how much ill feeling this gave rise to in almost every sector of society. Four pence per week for men and three for women with an employer's contribution and a government top-up of a further two pence per person bought sickness and disability benefit, free doctors, hospital and medicine, unemployment and maternity pay. The bill, which had been in preparation since 1907, was heavily amended at committee stage and then postponed for the coronation (Edward VII having died in 1910). At the coronation itself Lloyd George was booed by the families of Tory M.P.'s and by the peers. The Lords then wrecked the bill in committee, bringing a threat to swamp them with Liberal peers. In the face of this they reluctantly passed it, but it had to be guillotined in the Commons after further delays. It was perhaps not the best time for Lloyd George to be occupied with the investiture, coaching the prince in the Welsh sentences required for the ceremony. Then in 1912 a miners' strike and, from May to August, a dock strike, with the demand of a minimum wage, underlined the social unease over which the precarious government presided.

While the press and the middle class led resistance to the National Insurance scheme, Lloyd George had another battle to fight. Though himself an advocate of female suffrage, he was nevertheless a member of a government which had not brought it about, and hence a target for violence. His biographer John Grigg puts the matter clearly: ' . . . the Liberals' failure to enfranchise women was one of the worst blots on their record, and no amount of special pleading can excuse it.' Lloyd George was consequently heckled by suffragettes wherever he appeared in public, for instance at the National Eisteddfod at Wrexham that summer, and when he officially opened the Llanystumdwy village hall, which he had funded with his libel settlement, on 21st September.

On 17th January 1913 David Lloyd George was fifty. Frances Stevenson, then twenty-five, was half his age. Their affair was formalised on 21st. They regarded this as the day that they were married, although their actual wedding did not take place until after Margaret had died. As John Grigg again puts it: 'During most of their life together Lloyd George was, in reality, a bigamist.' It was lucky, he comments, that he lived when he did. The press turned a blind eye to almost anything short of divorce. Strangely that was still not acceptable. One of the reasons why Lloyd George did not divorce Margaret was probably that he loved, admired and had a need of her; another might well have been that it would have ruined his career.

A portrait of her then, in 1913, shows Frances Stevenson to have been a misty-eyed beauty with soft wavy hair. The contrast with the more homely, firm-featured Margaret is clear. John Grigg proposes that he needed both women. At any rate it was not difficult for him to keep them apart, since Margaret was content to stay mainly at Bryn Awelon, and in the meantime Sir George Riddell had built him a house at Walton Heath, near a golf course, where he went with Frances at the weekends.

Lloyd George's knack of charming women is difficult, at this distance, to explain. Asquith's daughter, interviewed in 1967, perhaps gives us a hint. 'He seemed to be guessing what I wanted him to say.' He then disconcerted her by turning to his table partner on the other side and applying the same charm. Whether or not he had a conscience is also a matter of debate. Balfour said of him: 'Principles mean nothing to him – never have. His mind doesn't work that way.' He was not, it may be gathered, universally liked or admired. Lord Northcliffe, the press baron, who knew him well, noted in an office memo: 'The emptiness of Lloyd George's head is becoming painfully apparent.'

This time was a hard one for him for another reason. Probably in complete innocence, but nevertheless with extreme rashness, he let himself become embroiled in a financial scandal. It was, says William, 'probably the most agonising period Dafydd ever experienced.' It appeared on the face of it that Lloyd George had profited from inside information when he bought one thousand shares in the American branch of Marconi which, two days later, increased in value by a hundred percent when the contract for government-owned wireless stations throughout the colonies was awarded to the British branch. In the inquiry which followed he was exonerated, and a Tory censure motion was defeated, but the demoralisation of the experience and the stain of suspicion remained. Moreover if the whole thing was an innocent, not to say naive, mistake, it made him, as Chancellor of the Exchequer, look remarkably foolish. To make things worse he rebought the shares he had sold, and in the end made a loss, revealing himself as a financial amateur.

In this period just before the war two issues dominated British politics: land reform, and Ireland. Lloyd George's intention on the first of these was to improve the lot of the rural poor. He campaigned for a minimum agricultural wage, and (for instance in his speech back in Pwllheli in December, 1913) for security for tenant farmers. His stance was basically anti-landlord, though it must be said that his socialism normally took a more positive form. He was not in general in favour of the relief of poverty solely by redistribution, so much as by capital growth. In this he laid the foundations of twentieth century social capitalism. His own form of socialism was distinctly paternalistic; he believed that 'the working class will never improve their position without the assistance of men in other walks of life . . . ' The arms race, particularly naval expansion, continued to obstruct his social policy, and he waged a running battle with his friend Winston Churchill who, now First Lord of the Admiralty, put the need for more battleships, in the face of German expansion, ahead of that of land reform. Back in Cricieth for Christmas, he gave a rash interview on the subject to the Daily Chronicle, for publication on New Year's Day, 1914.

The Irish question (which occurs in every chapter of British history) almost reached a sort of resolution that year, when a plan for home rule excluding some Ulster counties on a temporary basis reached the last stages of discussion in June, just as the Sarajevo assassination threw Europe into turmoil. The problem which was in the throes of being ironed out was what to do about the two mixed-religion counties of Tyrone and Fermanagh. The case of the four Protestant counties seemed clear enough: they could decide to opt out of independence by referendum. Whether or not to include in this system the other two was a question still being debated when Europe went to war. This event also overshadowed Lloyd George's second controversial budget, of April 1914, in which he sought to raise income tax by eleven percent (reduced in the end by cabinet intervention), inheritance tax by three, and supertax by a massive eighty percent.

In a way the war interrupted his career at a crucial stage, by checking his natural tendency to carry things to extremes. It has been speculated that he was at that point poised for failure. Certainly his, along with everyone's, fate was changed, by the fact that Germany failed to meet the midnight deadline on 4th August, to respect Belgian neutrality, thus obliging Britain to join in a pan-European shambles which has all the coherence, historically, of a pub brawl.

Lloyd George was against our involvement, but decided not to resign from the government. Instead he became a vital part of the coalition government, moving from the Treasury in May 1915 to become Minister of Munitions. It is ironic that in this role, and later as Secretary of State for War, he was directly responsible for the success of the offensive, while all the time advising Asquith to call it off, and campaigning for the removal of Haig, whom he memorably described as 'Brilliant, to the top of his boots.' The latter was later to have restored the balance somewhat when he said that 'history would show that the war had been won on the Western Front, in spite of Lloyd George.'

Haig was perceptive enough to see that he could not take Lloyd George at face value. He wrote in his diary, in January 1916: 'Lloyd George seems astute and cunning, with much energy and push but I should think shifty and unreliable.' When he went as War Minister to France, while the Somme battle was still raging, other writers noted his 'amazing energy' and 'great flow of words'. Even though his visits mainly concentrated on HQ's, and he saw little of the horror of action, he was of course aware of the terrible losses which Haig's conduct of the offensive were causing. When he got back after one visit he confided to Frances Stevenson: 'I was not meant to deal with things of war. I am too sensitive to pain and suffering . . . ' Conscription had become an issue from 1915, and it split the government. Volunteer recruitment was however falling, and compulsion became unavoidable. Lloyd George said in a speech in Conwy, a few days after it was introduced, that compulsory enlistment was only like compulsory taxation or compulsory education; compulsion, he said, somewhat disingenuously, is 'the voluntary decision of the majority . . . compulsion is simply organised voluntary effort.'

That was in May. On 1st July, the first day of the Battle of the Somme, twenty thousand British soldiers were killed. Some months later losses had amounted to 450,000, gains to a few miles of mud.

We think of Lloyd George today as a great British Prime Minister, but in fact he was a cabinet minister for eleven years before becoming Prime Minister for eight. That he became Prime Minister at all is the result of a number of unlikely chances, and was, at the time, rather against his will.

Part of the cause was the Easter Rising.

First, it was due to the Easter Rising that he was alive then at all. It had been his intention, as Munitions Minister, to go with Kitchener, then Secretary of State for War, to Russia, in June, 1916, to inspect munitions supplies. Asquith asked him to stay at home to handle the Irish situation. The ship Kitchener then went on alone was sunk off Orkney by a German mine, and Kitchener was drowned.

Secondly it was the Easter Rising which finally undermined confidence in Asquith's ability to govern, already severely weakened by conscription and the stalemate which the war seemed to have reached. There was more to it than this, of course. Asquith's mode of government, based on delaying decisions, was not suited to a time of war, and as 1916 wore on his physical powers visibly declined. His hands became shaky. As Roy Jenkins puts it: 'For the last ten or fifteen years of his life, at least, he was a fairly heavy drinker.' He was then aged sixty-four. To cap it all his son Raymond was killed in action on 15th September.

Seeing Asquith in the portrait in the Lloyd George museum we catch him in the rotundity of old age, double-chinned and pompous-looking. 'Good heavens,' remarked Lloyd George in Conwy, 'of what use would I have been if I had not differed from him?' The relationship between the two men is of interest, because it is clear that Asquith thought for the rest of his life that Lloyd George had in some way plotted his downfall. This is not borne out by the facts, and William says of his brother 'I know from what he told me . . . that he held his chief in high esteem.' He points out, however, that Asquith's 'injured personal vanity' was one of the factors which 'led to the break-up of the Liberal Party.'

We need not go into detail here about the pressure by the press and politicians which eventually forced Asquith to resign. It was long-drawn-out and bitter, and sustained by the fact that Asquith refused to believe that anyone else could form a government. Finally he went to Buckingham Pallace and resigned at 7.00 p.m. on December 5th; at 9.30 the King asked Bonar Law to form a government. He agreed on the condition that Asquith would serve, but the latter refused. By 6.00 p.m. the next day the matter was still unresolved. Law would not budge from his condition, nor Asquith accept it. 'So,' wrote the King in his diary, 'I sent for Lloyd George and asked him to form a Government, which he said he would endeavour to do.'

The results of this were inevitably precarious, and the fact of its taking place at all had far-reaching consequences. It meant that from the start the bulk of the Liberal Party, the 'Asquith Liberals', was essentially an anti-Lloyd George party. The government he formed contained few Liberals. He had always had a liking for coalitions, so this would not have worried him. Balfour, for instance, the Conservative ex-Prime Minister, was his

Foreign Secretary. Liberal ministers refused to serve under him, though he was well supported by back benchers. He formed a war cabinet of only five, in which he himself was the only Liberal. One of his first concerns, as ever, was to write home to Cricieth. To William he wrote: 'Tell Uncle Lloyd that he is responsible for putting me in this awful job.'

The war was going badly, when he took over. He at once confronted this issue in his own forthright way. His first speech to the House of Commons as Prime Minister has a ring to it which we now think of as Churchillian, though it is likely that the influence was the other way: 'I have always insisted on the nation being taught to realise the actual facts of this war.' He brought to the Premiership generally a presidential style which involved a greatly expanded secretariat through which he kept an eye on all departments. Unusually his cabinet included not only a strong labour representation but members from outside politics. His enlarged staff could not be housed in Whitehall's offices, and an encampment of huts grew up in the gardens of Numbers 10 and 11, known as 'The Garden Suburb'. His presidential style also included frequent absence from the House of Commons.

In 1916, even after the losses on the Somme, it was felt that the war should be pursued to its ultimate conclusion. It comes as some surprise to us to realise that it could have been ended sooner, but that Lloyd George, among others, thought it should not be. It was felt that outside interference, for instance by the United States, to bring it to a quick conclusion, would be favouring the Germans. Lloyd George saw the purpose of its continuation as being the prevention of its recurrence. 'This ghastliness must never be re-enacted on this earth,' he said in an influential interview with Roy Howard, president of the United Press of America.

In the event, of course, it was to recur, and within his own lifetime. In the meantime more than a thousand cemeteries testify to the cost. It has been estimated that it would take three and a half days for the dead to march past the cenotaph.

The supposed end to all wars was announced by Lloyd George to the House of Commons at 3.00 p.m. on November 11th, 1918.

During the last months of the war a silent film was made of Lloyd George's career. Remarkably it includes the last weeks even as they were still occurring, showing the triumphant troops returning home. There is no mention, however, that anyone had got killed; and perhaps it was because he felt too keenly that glorification of this war would at that moment be inappropriate that Lloyd George prevented the film being screened, even after its release had been advertised. There is little doubt that it was on his personal behalf that a solicitor arrived at the film company's offices and bought the cans of film for £20,000, paid in cash – the cost of making the film. It disappeared for the next seventy years, turning up by chance in the barn of Lloyd George's grandson, Lord Tenby, in Surrey, in 1992. That it was among family possessions is enough evidence that it was Lloyd George himself who bought the film.

There was civil unrest at the time. Indeed the second use of tanks, after their first use at the Somme, was on the streets of Glasgow, strike breaking. A general election (the first with a full franchise, at last including women), had returned the coalition government, in June. Lloyd George recognised that its immediate duty when the war was over was 'to make Britain a country fit for heroes to live in.' His brother William comments that this gospel was 'unaccompanied by any specific call to make the heroes fit for the Britain that was to be.' He was convinced, he said, that 'my brother was a disappointed and changed man after four years participation in a cruel and exhausting war . . . ' Uncle Lloyd had in the meantime died, in February 1917, without witnessing the victory.

In spite of its apparent success the coalition began to fall apart. A Tory resolution at the Carlton Club in October 1922 amounted to a declaration of independence, and Lloyd George at once resigned. He spent his time from then on on lecture tours in America and Canada, writing articles for the American press, and, of course, doing his duty as the continuing M.P. for Caernarvon Boroughs. In 1938, for instance, he came to Conwy to meet the objectors to the current road proposal, which would have run along the line of the quay, between the town and the river. He officiated at the unveiling of the 'white rabbit' memorial to Llandudno's connection with Alice in Wonderland, on the West Shore, on 6th September, 1933. During much of this time he was working on his War Memoirs, a massive document, the last volume of which was published in November 1936. This is often criticised as a distorted record of his attitude to the war, and as being unduly defensive. He continued to travel, in spite of deteriorating health. He was in Jamaica, for instance, when the abdication took place, in December 1936, returning the following spring.

Earlier that year, 1936, Lloyd George had taken his family to visit Hitler at Berchtesgaden; a home movie made of the event shows Uncle Adolf playing with the children. Although this seems somewhat shocking to us now, we have to remember that Lloyd George was by no means alone in falling for Hitler's charm. Indeed the phrase itself, 'Hitler's charm', is not the oxymoron it might to us appear to be, since his achievements in the early stages of his power owed not a little to force of personality. At any rate, Lloyd George was impressed.

He was at the time pressed to join the cabinet, but in the end his health

When Lloyd George returned to Llanystumdwy he bought an old farmhouse, Tŷ Newydd

The house was extended for him by the local architect Clough Williams-Ellis

did not permit a return to active politics. Indeed he went little to the House of Commons, though he remained an M.P., being returned with a 5000 majority in spite both of his ill health and the vast Conservative win which succeeded the failure of Ramsay MacDonald's Labour-led coalition in the mid-30's. He held his last great political meeting in Caernarfon Pavilion on 21st October, 1939. There was speculation that he would join Winston Churchill's coalition in 1940, but in the event he would not have been fit to do so and in any case was not asked.

At this time he was living at Churt, in Surrey, rather than in North Wales. He had built a new house there, which he called 'Bron y De'. 'It appeared,' writes his brother William, 'to be accepted as a matter of course that the heads of the family should have their separate headquarters.' Margaret (made a Dame at the end of the war) of course remained at Bryn Awelon. In the late autumn of 1940, however, she had been with William George's wife to a W.I. meeting at the Memorial Hall and walked the short distance up to Garthcelyn, William's house (a commanding, rather severe mansion, overlooking St Catherine's church), for tea, during which, helpfully going to the next room to answer the telephone, she slipped and fell on the parquet flooring, fracturing her hip. For eight weeks she was bedridden at Bryn Awelon, then unexpectedly died of a heart attack on 20th January, 1941. The country was deep in snow, Lloyd George struggling northwards through it, and the funeral took place in a wintry world. Though her life had been affected by the flow of events on a greater stage, the location of this end of it emphasises the small world which is Cricieth. Dame Margaret lies in the family vault now enriched by Goscombe John's memorial to Mair Eluned, only a little way below Mynydd Ednyfed, from whence she came into this story.

Lloyd George and Frances Stevenson were married quietly at Guildford registry office on 23rd October, 1943 (by which time he was eighty). 'The first I heard of my brother's second marriage,' writes William, 'to Miss Frances Stevenson, his private secretary for many years, was the announcement which appeared in the press the following day.' However it can hardly have been a surprise. Since they were living together anyway all that time, the main purpose of the marriage was perhaps to legitimise the daughter they had had together in 1930. This birth followed two earlier abortions, and although her existence was largely covered up and at one point implicitly denied by Frances, she represented the love-bond between them which could now take public form. For her part Jennifer Longford (as she became) called Lloyd George 'Taid' and understood she had been adopted by Miss Stevenson, and the truth only gradually emerged.

In 1944, rather to everyone's surprise, the Lloyd Georges left Surrey and returned to live in Llanystumdwy, which, sixty-four years earlier, he had noted that he had left without regret. He bought Tŷ Newydd, a substantial old farmhouse with some land, where he intended to set up a model farm and market garden. This enterprise never succeeded, but in the meantime he restored and enlarged the house, employing the already famous local architect, Clough Williams-Ellis.

Tŷ Newydd still shows the signs of this attention. A pleasantly sedate residence in bosky country up its own winding avenue, it has the air of a miniature chateau at the front, formal and simple; at the back it reveals a more spacious complex with a definite air of substance. Together with its complex of outbuildings it is now an institution providing writing courses.

William George noted changes in his brother on his return. 'Strangely enough, for the first time in our joint history, we did not seem to have much to say to one another' and 'the past, both his and mine, was obviously dead to him.' He was now declining physically. Attending the New Year's Day children's party at Berea Chapel he was 'hardly able to say a few words to the little children in front of him' – 'the man who . . . was able to play on the feelings of his audiences as a maestro plays his violin.' He had, it becomes clear, come home to Llanystumdwy to die.

Walking with William by the Dwyfor he pointed to the spot where he wished to be buried, and a stone on which he said he used to sit to admire the view up the river, which he wanted put on his grave. In the event the grave is a little downstream of where he wanted it, for some reason connected with the need to purchase the land quickly, but the boulder is the one he identified.

Two months before he died he relinquished his seat to take an earldom. It was thus that Frances Stevenson was, until her death in 1972, the dowager Countess Lloyd George. He died in the early evening of 26th March, 1945, at home at Tŷ Newydd, having lapsed into a coma. William and other family members were sitting waiting downstairs, while his daughter Megan and his wife each held one of his hands. Bizarrely the silence downstairs was broken by the BBC announcement of his death.

Llanystumdwy was thronged when the funeral took place, the Penybont woods crowded with people, some hundreds watching the ceremony of the burial from the far side of the river. Afterwards Frances commissioned Clough Williams-Ellis to design the monument surrounding the grave, a masterpiece, in its woodland setting, of sublime simplicity.

The title he chose, ennobled in the New Year's honours list that year, was Earl Lloyd George of Dwyfor, emphasising that this story ends where it began, and that the tumbling talkative Welsh river runs right through it.

The entrance to Lloyd George's grave was one of Clough's important local works

Clough Williams-Ellis designed the setting of Lloyd George's grave

Lloyd George lies buried by the river Dwyfor, under a stone on which he used to sit

Clough Williams-Ellis

From time to time there are people in Wales who are known only by their first names. No doubt at one time everybody would have known who you meant if you said 'Dylan'. In recent times Wynford, Cledwyn, Kyffin, have needed no further information. Of course it helps that the forenames are each distinctive. So it was with Clough. Everybody referred to him as that.

It is, as it happens, not a first name in origin, but the family name of a Flintshire family to whom he was related, the Cloughs of Plas Clough in the Vale of Clwyd, the ancestor of whom, a Denbigh glover, had become Queen Elizabeth I's agent in the Netherlands, and became the second of the four husbands of Catherine de Berwyn. Arthur Hugh Clough, the Victorian poet, was a descendant.

The Williams family were landowners resident at Plas Brondanw, and the Ellises had land at Glasfryn, on the Llŷn peninsular, both of which properties remained in the family when they intermarried. Glasfryn was in fact largely rebuilt by Clough's father. On his mother's side there were quarrying interests, and the family home in this case was none other than Tanrallt, built by William Madocks and at one time rented by Percy Bysshe Shelley. 'My mother was born and died there . . . ' Clough writes, 'a long low white Regency house spread along a high hillside terrace backed by cliffs and hanging beech woods . . . ' It had been 'lovingly restored' by his aunt Hilda Greaves, who lived there during his youth. Tanrallt is now, incidentally, a Steiner school.

Like several of the characters in this second volume Clough was born in England, and indeed carried out much of his career there, yet in the end he became essentially a man of North Wales. He was born at Gayton, in Northamptonshire, on 28th May, 1883, the fourth of six children, five of whom were boys. His father, who retired seemingly early from a college living, withdrew to the isolated world of Glasfryn, where Clough, from the age of four, had a sheltered and lonely upbringing.

The fact that he lived so long makes it slightly startling to think how long ago this was. Such a lifespan as his, of ninety-four years, falling as it did during a time of cataclysmic change, has curious historical effects. When I knew Clough he was in his eighties; he had known Lloyd George when Lloyd George was in his eighties; Gladstone was in his eighties when Lloyd George knew him. Remarking on his own experience of this strange back-looping temporal effect of a long life, Clough recalls that Bertrand Russell, his friend and neighbour, once told him that his grandmother used to have tea on Sunday afternoons with the widow of the Young Pretender, while his grandfather told him of conversations which he had with Napoleon on St Helena.

At the same time such a lifespan, falling at such a time, underlines the speed of change during our hectic century. Richard Haslam adeptly phrases it thus: ' . . . he saw straw laid in the streets of London to allay the suffering of the sick within from the rasp of carriage wheels on stone, and went on to help route the motorways through the English countryside sitting in a helicopter.' He saw his first car, Clough recalls, in the spring of 1895. He records a childhood London of crossing-sweepers, organ-grinders with monkeys, and dancing bears.

In 1897 the loneliness and isolation of Glasfryn was replaced by the frustrations and restrictions of Oundle. Clough did not take kindly, then or later, to academic life. Indeed it seems that he was not in any strict sense academically inclined. His friend Jonah Jones admits, in his memoir, that it was 'difficult to imagine eliciting any opinions from Clough on, say, Flaubert, Debussy or Rodin . . . ' He adds that Clough always seemed to be 'both civilised and educated, despite his frequent disclaimers'. Throughout his life Clough made much of his lack of education.

He left Oundle three years later, having gained one ascertainable thing from the experience. He had seen Kirby Hall, an Elizabethan ruined mansion. Possibly, as Jonah Jones remarks, had he not gone to Oundle he would not have had this seminal impression. The only other building which he cites himself as being formative is the great church at Clynnog Fawr.

After school he naturally went to Cambridge, where his father had been a fellow at Trinity, but his time there is passed over lightly in his own account, and he left quite soon, without a degree. This gesture to conventional education had convinced himself, at least, that he was unacademic by temperament.

Although, looking back, Clough can see that he was always at heart an architect, at the time he seemed to have little idea what he actually wanted to do. Unqualified, still young, with the single asset of a large number of influential relatives, he drifted through jobs in London, at first in engineering. It was something of a family speciality, as his father and at least one uncle had the habit of constructing machinery of their own invention. His mother's brother, of the Greaves family, the owners of Llechwedd slate mines, owned a steam-driven car, the first car in the area. In spite of these family traditions, however, his period of employment did not last, and as if quite suddenly, without much idea of how, he decided to become an architect.

He found the address of something called The Architectural Association in the London telephone book, and presented himself there. Rather to his surprise, it seems, he was enrolled. One thing which Clough was never short of was connections, and once his family had accepted that he was determined to become an architect they seem to have carefully steered him in the right direction. Through some such means he secured a commission while still attending the academy, and since that institution objected to his using its premises as his office he abruptly left it. He thus had, he was fond of saying, three months of formal architectural training. 'What, you took three months!' Lutyens himself later exclaimed. 'Why, I was through it all in three weeks.'

I think it is in fact central to Clough's achievements that he had almost no formal training, only, indeed, a minimum of education, the result of which was that his natural eye and sensitivity were free to flower in their own unrestricted way, unhampered by convention or notions of correctness. This is not to say that his work is only motivated by personal whim. His sense of tradition (as we shall see from the works themselves) is an ever-present force. So is the rigid discipline of strict craftsmanship. Anyone who would understand his approach to creativity must first study the drawings reproduced in Richard Haslam's invaluable book, where it becomes cumulatively apparent that at the foundation of his work lay a meticulous care and almost obsessive perfectionism. Whatever may appear wayward and fanciful, as we shall see much of the works at first sight do, in the underlying plan there is a sense of reverential respect for care and skill. Here perhaps lies the tension which is one of the prime qualifications of art.

His parents made him an allowance of £160 per year. Since this was even then scarcely a fortune we cannot help wondering at his rashness. Before he had even got his second commission he had opened an office off Gray's Inn Road. He seems to have had right from the start amazing confidence. Sure enough the first commission led to others, and he responded, with typical optimism, by moving his business to larger premises.

During this time, rather to our surprise, we find Clough to be behav-

Llangoed Hall, near Builth Wells, was Clough's first major commission

The design of this magnificent building shows his characteristic eye for detail

ing very much as a man-about-town. He mixed in high society, clubs, balls, dinner parties, country house weekends. There is a touch of despair in the hectic search for pleasure which involved the leisured classes in so much visiting and reception at salons in those years after the death of Victoria, and before the War. Clough seems to have immersed himself thoroughly in London society at this time, and to have forgotten all about Wales. One greatly influential effect of this period of his life is that in the course of it he met his future wife.

By his own account he had, sometimes with difficulty, avoided liaisons. Though never describable as handsome, he was tall and elegant, well connected, with a good background, and a keen dancer. That he fell for Amabel at once, and she for him, says much. It says that the long and happy, highly-successful marriage which ensued was based on an affinity best described as love.

This is worth mentioning, because it was also incidentally a sound career move. She was a Strachey, her father being the owner and editor of the Spectator, St Loe Strachey, High Sheriff, at the time, of Surrey. Amabel was brought up in a privileged but highly-cultured background, where family visitors would include Rudyard Kipling and the Sitwells.

They met by accident, not directly through the marriage-market which formed one of the springs of the country-house-weekend lifestyle of the Edwardians. It was to do with architecture. Strachey had set a competition, which Clough had entered. He failed to win the competition, but in the process of attending the gathering he caught sight of Amabel, not even knowing who she was. Thereafter they met whenever they could, and in 1915 they got married. It was to be, as Jonah Jones aptly puts it, 'one of the great long-lasting liaisons of the twentieth century'.

In 1908, when he was twenty-five, his father had given him Plas Brondanw, one of the family seats which, however, had been long neglected by them in favour of Glasfryn. It was at the time divided into tenements, but the bit of it which was available gave Clough and Amabel a Welsh base, and as the tenancies expired he took more and more of the house until it was all his, directing the improvements to it, rather in the manner of Madocks, from London, with occasional visits. At the same time he expanded his ownership of property around it, buying, for instance, Cnicht and the Moelwyns. Again as with Madocks, one wonders how all this is paid for.

Certainly during this period he was working, with some notable success. From a new office in Arundel House on the Victoria Embankment he embarked on what Richard Haslam regards as his twenty most productive years, a span which however was interrupted by the First World War.

His style at this time, much influenced by Lutyens, can best be described as Arts and Crafts. A touch of modernism was always playing at the back of his approach to tradition, although he never fully took to the modern movement, always retaining a hint of the influence of Victorian classicism which overshadowed his formative period. If this summary of his early style seems to be saying that Clough as an architect was a bit of everything, that is not too inaccurate. What he started with, and retained, is a glorious eclecticism.

One thing he seems always to have had in abundance is enormous luck. His first major commission came about as a result of a chance meeting on a train. Llangoed Hall, described as one of the last Edwardian country houses, the first substantial country house to be built by Clough in this, the first phase of his career, was started in 1913. Its construction was interrupted by the War, but he came back to finish it in 1919. Many years later he was instrumental in preventing its demolition, and it is now (just off the A470 in mid Wales) a hotel, having been saved by Sir Bernard Ashley.

A stately pile wedded to an old manor house, ten miles out of Builth on the Brecon side, Llangoed is run by its present management in the fine style of English stately-home hotels. It houses a fine collection of late nineteenth and early twentieth century paintings and drawings. On a landing at one end is a set of Clough's architectural drawings for 'alterations at Llangoed Castle', in which his consummate eye for detail is revealed in sketches for windows, staircases and doors. Grand was the plan, grand the result, in pillared gallery and pedimented porch. Outside the Hall proclaims a consistent neo-Gothic style, except for some rather startling tall Tudor chimneys, a reference to the Jacobean original. Did it, one wonders, look modern at the time? There is little about it that would strike us as daring now.

That this should have been the work of an untried and untutored thirty-one year old is staggering, and it points at once to Clough's abiding talent, his supreme self-confidence. He always believed, without question, in his ability to do things – it never occurred to him to doubt it. This, Llangoed proclaims, was the case from the start.

The success of the completed work, after the war, formed the beginning of his career. His gaining of the commission itself, just before the outbreak, meant (at least in his eyes) that by the time the First World War started he was established. His determination to enlist is all the more surprising. Leaving his first major commission unfinished he avidly set about finding a regiment. The war fever which was sweeping the country at the time is the only possible explanation. Jonah Jones comments that everyone thought the whole affair would be over by Christmas. 'Indeed, men were worried it might be all over before they could play their part.' Nobody, at that stage, could have foreseen the Battle of the Somme.

Having moved rapidly between a number of regiments, he joined the Welsh Guards as soon as they were formed, later transferring, seemingly out of curiosity to the equally new Tank Corps. Clough makes light of his time at the front: 'I know of no tedium so utterly blistering as that of routine trench warfare in a relatively quiet sector . . . I sent home for my water-colours and did sketches . . . ' One of the incidentals of his war was his marriage. Seeking his commanding officer's permission for this, he was asked what he wanted for a wedding present. 'A ruin,' he replied, with the result that on the hill behind Plas Brondanw a seemingly ancient keep looks out over the intricate Welsh landscape. A closer look displays the gleeful sense of fun always apparent in his work. This, the 'Outlook Tower', was his wedding present from his fellow officers.

Amabel was a nurse during the war, so that the newly-weds had to try to arrange for their terms of leave to coincide in order to meet at all. They did however manage to spend some time at Plas Brondanw, and indeed their first daughter Susan was born while her father was still sporadically in the trenches.

Returned from his uneventful war he plunged back into private practice, after an unsuccessful three months as a civil servant. Llangoed was finished, and evidently with some time to spare Clough began to involve himself in planning and conservation. The Council for the Preservation of Rural England had just been formed, with his keen support, and he himself became appointed chairman of the Design and Industries Association, which he proceeded to make into an active and influential force. Clough claimed the next event came 'out of the blue', but once again we see the combination of his fruitful luck with a network of connections.

Clough had been asked by his father-in-law, the owner and editor, to write an article on Stowe for the Spectator. The seat of the Dukes of Buckingham, the palace had received the attentions of architects and designers as distinguished as Vanburgh, William Kent and Capability Brown. Recently it had fallen into decline, and was in fact now for sale. After the article appeared Clough was approached by the intending purchaser, who planned to turn it into a school. He wanted him to design and oversee the conversion. Although this all makes perfect sense, it is not, we feel, the sort of thing which happens to most of us.

Bits were sold off to pay for the work. In the process a statue of Freya found its way to Portmeirion, where it stands below the Dolphin. The Grand Avenue itself was to be sold for housing, and on an impulse Clough bought it himself to save it. Not for the first or last time one wonders at his financial standing and the risks he took with it. Presumably he was temporarily in debt, reliant on being bailed out by well-wishers. That was in 1921; during the next few years work proceeded on the new school buildings.

Clough had the difficult task of marrying new work to historic architecture and landscape. His work at Stowe is not always judged a success. John Piper thought he had 'rather wrecked' the place. The change in scale, from the extravagance of Vanburgh to the demands of the time, was necessitated, of course, by sheer financial constraint. Jonah Jones, polite as ever, has the possible reservation 'that there is a lightness of touch about it that does not accord well with the sheer weight of the incumbent High Baroque'. It is this lightness of touch which we shall come to recognise as being Clough's trademark, the inability to resist having a bit of fun, and it is perhaps this playfulness which, if anything, has prevented him from being taken seriously as a first-class architect. He referred to it himself, writing about Portmeirion, as a light-opera approach. It is at the same time the thing for which some love, and others hate, his work.

The conversion of Stowe led to commissions for other decaying palaces. Ashridge, for instance, a Gothic Revival pile, he converted to become the Bonar Law College for aspiring conservative politicians. Now, in the 1930's, Clough and Amabel, with three children, lived in Hampstead, surrounded by modernist artists and writers. Hampstead in the 1930's is another of those golden ages, like Edwardian society London.

Clough, in spite of his context, was not himself a modernist architect. The ideals of proportion and elegance to which he adhered belonged more to the Palladian style. He was, Richard Haslam points out, 'too old by half a generation' to take to modernism easily. Jonah Jones sees him, probably correctly, as the last of the Palladians. 'Palladio was really at the base of much of Clough's work'.

Living in this rarified atmosphere, and themselves a distinguished part of it, they of course knew everyone. Clough gives the slightly unfortunate impression in his autobiography that he was not terribly interested in other people. He contents himself with a long list of famous names, without telling us, tantalisingly, what they were like. Through H.G. Wells he met 'Rose Macaulay, Arnold Bennett, Maynard Keynes . . . Harold Laski, Baroness Budberg, Charlie Chaplin, Elsa Lancaster, Philip Guedalla, Miles Malleson, the Huxleys, and I don't know who besides.'

He was himself, by now, the author of two books (the first a collaboration with his literary wife). 'The Pleasures of Architecture' came out in 1924, lamenting the decline of standards, which, I suppose, every age in turn feels inclined to do. It is a book primarily, however, about pleasure, as the title implies, and aesthetic expression of belief. The second book, 'England and the Octopus', was very much his own.

Published in 1928, it has much to teach even today. It has been well described, by Clough himself among others, as an angry book. A successful new edition came out in 1975.

One thing that is slightly startling is the realisation that Clough had forgotten, for the time being, about his inheritance. Why 'England', rather than 'Britain'? The profits from the book were donated to the Council for the Preservation of Rural England, not Wales. He refers from time to time, in give-away phrasing, to 'the English people'. The book is, in fact, essentially about the condition and ethos of being English, a concept which not everybody would find it easy to comprehend. It is perhaps something to do with chronic nostalgia: ' . . . never again will England be an island of unsmirched country and ordered towns'. 'England', it seems, is forever something which can only be evaluated in a past tense.

It is hard to write a book on this subject, given its very nature, without occasionally sounding élitist; and it must be said that Clough does not sound as if he would have minded failing to avoid this. He refers to 'mean and perky little houses that surely none but mean and perky little souls should inhabit with satisfaction', pointing up the paradox of an avowedly socialist book written to protect middle-class standards. 'We plant trees in the towns and bungalows in the country, thus averaging England out into a dull uneventfulness . . . ' He is undoubtedly right in pointing to overpopulation as the greatest threat to the environment, and to the decline in the birth-rate as being the most hopeful sign of improvement. Once again however to assume that the romantic view of nature is axiomatic, that wilderness is the desired aim, is to miss the point of the essential interrelatedness of place and population.

Much of 'England and the Octopus', despite these cavils, is of seminal and permanent importance. It led the way into the modern environmental movement. It makes the crucial point that we are all responsible: 'Everyman is answerable'. Though it is government's duty to 'protect that natural heritage', the duty of the individual is to lobby to this end. Education is the ultimate answer. One cannot possibly quarrel with sentiments such as these.

Between the wars Clough took to yachting, in a somewhat happy-go-lucky, not to say foolhardy way. What started as a thirst for adventure in

Plas Brondanw, an old family residence, became the Williams-Ellises North Wales home

The garden is a personal expression of the architect's taste

due course became the medium of a quest. He started to look for what he then thought must be an island site, to provide the setting for his ideal village, 'to show others what I thought could be done'. About this time, on a trip to Italy, he had discovered Portofino. No doubt he always had this form of place in mind.

Islands proved consistently unsuitable, usually too remote to build on economically. How he came to find the ideal place not five miles from his Welsh home, the nearest bit of coastline, is another example of his incredible luck.

Portmeirion in the end eludes explanation. He himself classed the questions about it as three, 'Why?', 'How?' and 'When?', and failed to give a clear answer to any of them. As to 'When?' all we can do is point to a genesis during this period of search, in which the idea became ever more clear in his head. The actual dating of its gradual growth 'is not so easily disposed of as I have never kept a diary', and all his records were destroyed in a fire. It is known, however, that he started work on what was then an overgrown jungle in 1926.

What happened has the air of high improbability, but such things did actually happen to Clough. An 'absentee uncle', Sir Osmond Williams of Deudraeth Castle, asked Clough if he knew anyone who would buy his coastal property known as Aber Ia. The tenant was described as a 'strange old lady', who, it turned out, had lived in that secluded valley for many years as a recluse. Her demise raised the question of what to do with it. Clough saw it initially with the eyes of a yachtsman, as being the ideal port for Plas Brondanw. That house had itself once been on the sea, but had become marooned by Madocks' and other landowners' reclamation, a 'misguided enterprise', Clough thought, ' . . . the whole business, as I hold, most deplorable.' He would, if he could, have reversed it. Meanwhile the result was that Aber Ia was the nearest coast to Plas Brondanw.

It only gradually seems to have dawned on him that this was exactly what he had been looking for. He had somehow set his sights on an island, but a coastal valley was even better. He cleared the jungle, opened up the old house, and set about building Portmeirion.

How we wonder once again was all this financed? 'My professional earnings . . . outstripped my modest expectations.' In other words he was doing quite well. As a result 'I realised that I could indeed do it.' The project was, moreover, from the start, overtly commercial. Its market was 'unashamedly tourism'. Upmarket tourism, certainly. 'A holiday retreat for the more discerning.' Indeed it had a touch of an élitist stance, recognising the need for protection from 'the spreading infection of the bunga-

Portmeirion, fulfilment of a life-long dream, is of course Clough's most famous artefact

The modernist Morannedd cafe at Cricieth is a striking example of his versatility

low virus'. In accordance with the need for the project to pay for itself the first thing to do was open the house as a hotel, and this took place at Easter in 1926. People came, during the early years, out of curiosity and because of its owner's reputation. By the 1970's Portmeirion was receiving a hundred thousand visitors a year. There was room – 'There is seldom more than an agreeable sense of the place being alive and used'. And he was glad to see them. 'Personally I like figures in my landscape . . .'

To Clough it was the fulfilment of a lifelong dream. Since he was a child he had felt that 'some day, somewhere, I would assuredly erect a whole group of buildings on my own chosen site for my own satisfaction . . . ' Others recognised that he had succeeded in achieving something truly his. 'No one else,' writes Jonah Jones, who is responsible for the many inscriptions, 'could have built Portmeirion'. Others would have been tempted to make it more ordered, 'more pure'. Lewis Mumford described it as a 'deliberately irresponsible reaction against so much that passes as modern architecture, a folly in the eighteenth century sense.' Clough lists the features he himself saw as being its essence, describing the visit of Frank Lloyd Wright. The great man seemed 'to see the point of all my wilful pleasantries, the calculated naiveties, eye-traps, forced and faked perspectives, heretical constructions, unorthodox colour mixtures and general architectural levity.' It is never forgotten that he called his attitude to it 'a gay, light-opera sort of approach.' James Morris, writing in Horizon, is bewitched by this spell against his better judgement: 'I am not myself much addicted to whimsy in architecture . . . ' but revisiting Portmeirion 'I always have to admit that I am wrong again, and that this little false village is a proper work of art and intellect . . . I can only express my own reaction – something between a scoff, a gasp and an ecstasy.' The important thing to remember, I think, is that Clough regarded the business of having fun as being a worthwhile and wholly respectable enterprise. 'It is serious,' I wrote of Portmeirion in "Portrait of North Wales", 'to the extent that all good jokes are serious.'

The existence of Portmeirion may have inclined him to spend more time in Wales, but it was I think Hitler's bombs which proved more compulsive. Clough and Amabel moved to Plas Brondanw at the start of the war, and there they then stayed, to become indeed one of North Wales' great institutions.

Although he had of course done work in the area before that, his permanent presence here left its mark on the landscape most noticeably from that time on. It is perhaps unfair to mention the building on Snowdon summit, erected in 1934, which was dictated by the difficulties of the site.

It is perhaps his one lapse from the habit of giving pleasure. If we want to understand his mature period we should look at what he did to Plas Brondanw itself, and more particularly his garden.

This is both a personal statement and an expression of the mind of an architect, all organised lines of vista, highly formal yet still expressive of a gleeful sense of fun. That quality is apparent too in the 'Outlook Tower' already mentioned, and in his treatment of the house itself. Almost incredible flights of fancy, combined with a reckless eclecticism, enabled him to blend Italianate arches and balconies with Welsh eighteenth century classicism. Fanciful, whimsical, perhaps, flights of sheer fantasy, an often brilliant soaring of the spirit is released as his seemingly limitless imagination was given its freedom, making his best work the cause of magical delight. It was, one feels, all for pleasure, all for fun. Why (his work implies) should it not be?

One of the best examples of this attitude of his mature, North Wales period, is a conversion carried out for his friend Christabel Lady Aberconway on a hillside above Cwm Croesor. Here a serious piece of industrial history, the 'Drum House' of a cable railway, has been converted into a folly in the sky, Cnicht on one side bounding the horizon, on the other the huge sweep of reclaimed Traeth Mawr, as far as the embankment and the open sea. Befitting perfectly Clough's happy attitude, it proclaims itself instantly as the perfect place for a perfect party. And such a party there once was, when Christabel's family and friends gathered there one summer day for her eightieth birthday. Jonah Jones, who was there, remembers it as 'The View Party. 'As we sat on the steep grassy slope below the Drum House, quaffing wine and gossiping, spread out below us was Traeth Mawr and the Cob . . .' How different that view would have been, we cannot help thinking, and Clough no doubt on that occasion thought, if Madocks had not drained it. A silver sheet of sea, or a tidal gleam of estuarial silt.

During the late 1930's Clough had designed a number of seaside houses, such as Coed y Castell in Deganwy, built in 1939 for Dr and Mrs Talbot in a fine setting directly under Maelgwn's fortress on the Vardre. The metal windows which he often favoured in this case lack the horizontal bars which give a similar house of his design, Sheraton in Craigside, Llandudno, a definitely 1930's look. In the Deganwy one they form two eighteen foot bays which give the whole interior an airy, light-filled atmosphere which creates an immediate sense of pleasure, while the house outside proclaims its status with a firm sense of outlook across what were then its own grounds to Conwy Bay. Both houses have his characteristic round roofs on their bays. The use of metal windows (even in the almost self-effacing church hall at Pentrefelin, which, however, gives its maker away by its varied roof pitches and splayed eaves, lightly ornamental bell-tower and the gratuitous flourish of a wooden soffit) reminds us that Clough in fact relished new materials, often using them to create a traditional effect. A good example is the summer house he built for Christabel Lady Aberconway at Maenan Hall, the 'crystal room', where moulded aluminium and perspex form a gracefully arched roof.

Back at Pentrefelin, behind the church, it is interesting to see how he succeeded in directing his natural playfulness to perform in a serious setting. The grandiose parsonage which he designed there (now very sympathetically extended) has its telltale round roofed porch, flared corners on the roofs of even the dormers. Even serious subjects such as this and the church hall are given a pleasing lift by unexpectedly decorative details. As Richard Haslam put its: his works 'have a brilliance, simplicity and charm which shine through the grimmest of centuries . . .

Clough was frustrated at now being too old to take a direct part in the war, which also held up work on Portmeirion. His son Christopher was killed (aged 23) in action at Monte Cassino. His natural exuberance was stifled not just by this tragedy but by the austerity and restriction of the time. Earlier in the war he had defied these. On the occasion of his daughter Charlotte's twenty-first birthday, Clough, who was, as Jonah Jones put it, 'especially addicted to firework displays' and who somehow had a store of fireworks saved from before the war, held a party in the vast underground slate cavern at Llechwedd (owned by his mother's family), where he could hold a suitably grand firework display without attracting enemy attention.

After the war he was back in prominence, hard at work on Portmeirion and in the conservation movement. He was already in his sixties, and eminent, when Lloyd George, in his eighties, moved back to Llanystumdwy. 'I fell,' he writes, 'under the spell of his most subtly exercised charm, as indeed did almost everyone else.' He renovated Tŷ Newydd for the great man, and built the charming cottage up the hill to house his bailiff, the ostensible modesty of which is undermined by its quaint neat porch and characteristic flared gables. Later, after Lloyd George's death, he was to be responsible not only for the grave itself but the museum and (in 1970) the memorial in Westminster Abbey, carved by Jonah Jones.

One of the innovations in the aftermath of the second war was the concept of New Towns. Clough had already praised, in 'England and the Octopus', the new 'garden suburbs' such as those of Welwyn, Letchworth and Hampstead. Now he found himself in a rare public position, and one

Clough designed a number of houses in North Wales in the 1930 such as Coed y Castell in Deganwy and Sheraton in Craig y Don

of some considerable responsibility, appointed Chairman of the Stevenage Corporation.

There is some irony in this. He was opposing plans to flood Cwm Croesor, and all his life had railed against the draining of Traeth Mawr. The two objections being of different sorts, their common element must be a tendency to resist change. How then could he contemplate imposing a whole new community on natural countryside?

There were some who were not at all happy about this.

One of these, in an episode which carries a resonance which apparently left Clough unmoved, was E.M. Forster. 'The Rooks' Nest', Forster's model for Howard's End, was about to become part of Stevenage New Town. Forster was so concerned about this that he got in touch with the Administrator, with the result that Clough (who filled that role as well as that of Chairman) drove him down there to inspect. They had tea with the current tenants. 'An unforgettable experience, as never in my life have I been received with such implacable hostility.' It is incredible to us that he mentions Forster only as a name, and gives us no view of what it was like to go on a long drive with him. It seems, as so often with his mention of famous names, as if his focus of interest was not on them. We catch another tantalising glimpse of Forster later, in an even more inviting setting, when, at Bertrand Russell's ninetieth birthday party, he (out of politeness, perhaps, or lassitude) acquiesced at what Clough and others had done to Stevenage. What a chance to sketch in an impression of that event has here been missed. To be present there and say no more about it is little short of literary blasphemy.

Clough, faced with the hostility of Howard's End's new tenants, disowned the blame for Stevenage. 'I had nothing whatsoever to do with the choice of Stevenage.' He argues on the 'greater good' principle. 'Nothing I could say in any way abated my hostess's indignation that blazed away at me across the startled tea-cups. To my surprise' (he adds somewhat naively) 'I got no word of support from Forster . . . '

We get another merely photographic view of fame around this time when he went to Chartwell to visit Churchill. The latter 'lay in bed under a top-dressing of papers and telephones with secretaries discreetly popping in and out, but without interrupting our talk,' and this at mid-morning. 'He handed me a prodigious cigar some eight inches long with his name on the band;' but later: 'as for the fabulous cigar, having popped it into my breast pocket, I clean forgot about it until undressing that night, when I found the poor thing broken in two with neither fit to smoke nor to cherish as an heirloom.' One may marvel indeed at the outlook of someone who is given a Churchill havana by Churchill, and then forgets

Clough's association with Christabel Aberconwy gave rise to his design of the Drum House, above Cwm Croesor, and the 'crystal room' summerhouse at Maenan Hall

about it.

His autobiography, 'Architect Errant', from which much of this later information is derived, is an old man's book, written in his eighties, full of disorganised rambling reminiscence. For a book written by an architect it shows a curious lack of form, balance or structure. It has (as others have pointed out) an almost complete lack of dates, which adds to its vague feeling of half-remembrance. One notices also a studied, but not always successful, attempt to preserve a tone of modesty.

Part of the reason for a shortage of hard facts is that all Clough's records and many of his drawings were lost in the fire which consumed Plas Brondanw in 1951. It was only by the fortunate accident that they were getting up early to catch a train that he and Amabel were not consumed as well. The fire started in the ground-floor library, and by the time they became aware of it it was out of control. Clough and Amabel stood on the lawn in their dressing gowns and watched the house reduced to a shell. It took two years to rebuild.

Clough continued working into his old age, lecturing abroad, in Germany and the Middle East, in his seventies, still sailing and travelling throughout the 1960's. He received the C.B.E. in 1958, aged seventy-five, and finally, of course, in 1972, a knighthood. A mild heart attack hardly affected his disposition to celebration. 'Oh, one of those things,' remarked Bertrand Russell. 'I had one forty years ago in China and was none the worse for it.' Both his eightieth and ninetieth birthday parties were magnificent affairs. Finally, however, he broke his femur. Jan Morris came to visit him on what turned out to be his death bed. Clough remarked that because he didn't trust anybody to get his obituary right he had written it himself, and handed it to her. She could hardly tell him that she had in fact already written the official one for the Times.

Towards the end, in April of 1978 in which he died, Jonah Jones and Richard Haslam helped him outside into the spring sunshine. Clough chose that occasion to announce 'I've decided after all these years that I'm an atheist.'

He died that month at the age of ninety-four. To a large extent his unchangingness over those years has led to a stereotyping process, which extends to people's attitude to his work. Yet although there is always something about a Williams-Ellis building which makes one sure it is by him – a matter, probably, of approach, rather than style, a visible sense of fun, of taking pleasure in appearances – his style itself was by no means stereotyped, as the work of some architects all too plainly is. Indeed it varies very considerably over the course of his long career. Clough, whose life spanned several high periods of British architectural history, clearly moved with the times. His use of modern materials already mentioned is one of his trademarks.

Take the Moranedd cafe, for instance, on the beach at Cricieth: a 1950's building in an Art Deco style, vigorously, almost stridently, uncompromising in its modernity, all window lines and flat roof, its severity only partly relieved by the open arms, facing the sea, of its 'boomerang' form. The dining room extension of the hotel at Portmeirion itself has a firm touch of unapologetic modernism about it as well.

Nothing, on the face of it, could be more of a contrast with these later works than his first personal statement, Llangoed Hall. Here the sureness of touch which makes it so suitable now to its present luxurious purpose is of the grand orchestral mode, all columned corridors and broad flights of stairs. Times and visions had changed between, and Clough's eye changed with them.

It is easy to overlook his versatility. To some extent the view of him as favouring the old-fashioned does, of course, reflect his own preferences. 'He was never an innovative artist,' writes Jan Morris in the Times obituary, 'He built in a genre of romantic classicism, sometimes weakened by whimsy and artifice, and recognised little merit in any architectural style since the Georgian.' This, however, is perhaps not the whole story. It is tempting also to see him mainly through the filter of Portmeirion, which is representative of his views largely because it is a synthesis of styles and forms, rather than for any consistency. Portmeirion is, of course, his main memorial, and the best way, still, to come to understand him. As Jan Morris, again, says elsewhere, 'with all its faults and all its merits, it is himself perpetuated . . . ' To concentrate too much on this, however, could be to end up seeing him exclusively in local terms. Richard Haslam wonders to what extent that is his place: 'ultimately he seems both a national architectural figure, and part of the flora and fauna of North Wales which he worked so long to make better known and more glorious . . . '

He described himself, in his eightieth birthday speech, as 'congenitally deviationist', and thought he would be best known for 'tub-thumping all over the place'. He saw his work as too light to be important, referring to 'Portmeirion and such like trivia'. 'No great work of mine,' he said, 'stands out against the sky in splendour to excite men's wonder.'

It has become conventional, to some extent, to follow this judgement, and see him as something of a curiosity, diverting attention from the work to the somewhat eccentric character. Thus much is made, in all the memoirs, of the man himself. 'Yet for all these accomplishments,' writes Jan Morris at the end of the Times obituary, 'he was remarkable chiefly for himself . . . Clough Williams-Ellis was his own best work, splendid in all proportions . . . ' 'He was himself,' writes Richard Haslam, 'a remarkable invention . . . '

It is true that he himself encouraged such an attitude, maintaining an unchanging physical image. Being so tall and gaunt anyway, he had only to top this off with long white hair and a fanciful hat to be an instantly recognisable icon. The tweed plus-fours with high yellow stockings became a trademark, though I imagine they started in a previous era as a functional and effective form of costume. Out of doors he wore a well-cut navy-blue serge donkey jacket, essentially a workman's coat, of which as a young man I was greatly envious.

I regret to this day not having got round to asking him where he got it.

A cottage at Llanystumdwy and the church hall at Pentrefelin show the flair with which Clough could make even the humblest and simplest structures beautiful

119

Epilogue

One thing that will be clear by now, now that we have gone all the way from the Dark Ages to the present day, is that a number of persistent themes thread through the relationship between the land of North Wales and its central figures. One is that all the characters in the two volumes of this book have had to deal in one way or another with their neighbours, whether across the Irish Sea or inland. I suppose we all define ourselves to some extent by contrast, and on a geographical level this takes the form of territorial exclusion. Competition between North Wales and its landward neighbour, originally Mercia, by then less precisely known as 'England', ran through our earlier chapters. What has significantly changed by the time we come to the second volume, in fact after the lifetime of Sir John Wynn, is that our characters are increasingly able to take part in both worlds. Madocks, the first Marquess, and most obviously Lloyd George in fact took roles of varying significance in the government of Britain as a whole, with Sir Clough being a leading figure in English as well as Welsh design and conservation. It became no longer possible to see their lives and careers in an exclusively Welsh context.

Yet they would (and this is another survival of a persistent theme) have been proudly insistent that they belonged to a long Welsh lineage. Indeed we find that Sir Clough claimed to be able to trace his ancestry to Gruffydd ap Cynan, the great-grandfather of Llywelyn the Great and a distant descendant of Maelgwn Gwynedd. Part of the explanation for this persistent theme of ancestry is that North Wales is a settled country, still (as you cannot be involved in farming here without discovering) conscious of the ties of extended family groups.

It is in fact heartening to find so much continuity over so great a time.

Bibliography

Chapter 1:
A.H. Dodd, *A History of Caernarvonshire* (Caernarvonshire Historical
  Society)
Elizabeth Beazley, *Madocks and the Wonder of Wales* (Faber & Faber)
Thomas Pennant, *Tours in Wales*

Chapter 2:
The Marquess of Anglesey, *One Leg* (Leo Cooper)
Sir Walter Scott, *Life of Napoleon Buonaparte*
J.G. Lockhart, *The History of Napoleon Buonaparte* (Dent)
Philip Guedalla, *The Duke* (Hodder & Stoughton)
A.H. Dodd, *Bishop Lewes Bayly*, (Transactions of the Caernarfonshire
  Historical Society XXVIII, 1967)

Chapter 3:
William George, *My Brother and I*
John Grigg is the author of the standard multi-volume biography,
  and also of *Lloyd George and Wales* (National Library)

Chapter 4:
Jonah Jones, *Clough Williams-Ellis, the Architect of Port Meirion,
  A Memoir* (Seren)
Richard Haslam, *Clough Williams-Ellis* (reproductions of the
  architectural drawings from 1905 to 1970 (Academy Editions)
Clough Williams-Ellis, *England and the Octopus; Architect Errant;
  Portmeirion, the Place and its Meaning*
Jan Morris, *Pleasures of a Tangled Life*

Acknowledgements

The author wishes to thank the Marquess of Anglesey, Mr & Mrs Carey-
Evans, Mrs Enid Williams, and the management of Llangoed Hall Hotel
for their assistance in his research; and Mrs Mary Meldrum for her assistance in correcting the proofs.

REGIONS OF WALES – LOCAL HISTORY/GUIDES ▷

'THE STORY OF . . . ' SERIES

Wendy Hughes interweaves history, tales and events with attractive and interesting locations that will captivate and excite the visitor, leaving the reader breathless and surprised as she turns back the tide of time and glimpses into each century.

- **THE STORY OF GOWER.**
  88 pp. incl illustrations *ISBN 0-86381-217-1; £3.75*

- **THE STORY OF PEMBROKESHIRE**
  100 pp. *ISBN 0-86381-253-8; £3.75*

- **THE STORY OF BRECKNOCK**
  104pp. by Donald Gregory *ISBN 0-86381-316-X; £4.25*

- **RADNORSHIRE – A HISTORICAL GUIDE**
  - Donald Gregory. Radnorshire in many respects is Wales in a microcosm – hilly, wild, beautiful and small with the past ever present. 168 pp. *ISBN 0-86381-284-8; £4.50*

- **TWO BRIDGES OVER MENAI**
  - Robin Richards. History of the construction of the bridges across the Menai Straits. *ISBN 0-86381-387-9; £2.75*

- **THIS VALLEY WAS OURS**
  - Eileen M. Webb. History of Nant Gwrtheyrn as remembered by one of the village's children *ISBN 0-86381-428-X; £7.50*

- **TOMOS O ENLLI/TOMOS THE ISLAND MAN**
  with illustrations by Kim Atkinson. *ISBN 0-86381-565-0; £4.00*

- **THE OLD VILLAGES OF DENBIGHSHIRE AND FLINTSHIRE**
  Dewi Roberts. *ISBN 0-86381-562-6; £4.95*

- **ALL IN A DAY'S WORK**
  RAF Mountain Rescue in Snowdonia 1944-46 - David W. Earl. *ISBN 0-86381-554-5; £4.95*

- **THE HISTORY OF THE RIVER DEE**
  - Mike Griffiths. *ISBN 0-86381-553-7; £7.95*

THE MICHAEL SENIOR SERIES

– A widely published historian with a series of well written volumes about different areas of North Wales:

- **THE CONWY VALLEY – ITS LONG HISTORY**
  48pp. *ISBN 0-86381-035-7; £1.50*

- **LLANDUDNO'S STORY**
  32pp. *ISBN 0-86381-391-7; £1.75*

- **ANGLESEY – THE ISLAND'S STORY**
  64 pp. *ISBN 0-86381-389-5; £2.75*

- **CONWY – THE TOWN'S STORY**
  32 pp. *ISBN 0-86381-345-3; £1.95*

- **CAERNARFON – THE TOWN'S STORY**
  32 pp. *ISBN 0-86381-346-1; £1.95*

- **LLŶN – THE PENINSULA'S STORY**
  48 pp. full of illustrations; *ISBN 0-86381-443-3; £1.95*
- **MEIRIONNYDD'S STORY**
  64 pp. full of illustrations; *ISBN 0-86381-442-5; £1.95*
- **ERYRI – THE STORY OF SNOWDONIA**
  ISBN 0-86381-549-9; £2.75
- **THE CROSSING OF THE CONWY**
  - Michael Senior. From prehistoric times to the new tunnel. 112 pp. *ISBN 0-86381-191-4; £3.75*
- **NORTH WALES IN THE MAKING**
  - Michael Senior. A guide to the area's early history. Hard-back. 128 pp. *ISBN 0-86381-322-4; £9.75*

WELSH HISTORY/PEOPLE

Donald Gregory's Series –Guides to historical locations with a brief history:

- **WALES BEFORE 1066 – A GUIDE**
  144 pp. maps/illustrations; *ISBN 0-86381-396-8; £4.00*
- **WALES BEFORE 1536 – A GUIDE**
  160 pp. maps/illustrations; *ISBN 0-86381-250-3; £4.50*
- **WALES AFTER 1536 – A GUIDE**
  156 pp. maps/illustrations; *ISBN 0-86381-318-6; £4.95*
- **THE BATTLES OF WALES**
  - Dilys Gater. An account of battles on Welsh soil. 128 pp. *ISBN 0-86381-178-7; £3.00*
- **HISTORIC SHIPWRECKS OF WALES**
  - Dilys Gater, 136 pp. *ISBN 0-86381-216-3; £3.50*
- **THE YOUNG REPUBLICANS**
  - 'Gweriniaethwr'. A record of the Welsh Republican Movement. 184 pp. *ISBN 0-86381-362-3; £7.50*
- **THE DAY BEFORE YESTERDAY**
  - Donald Gregory. Historical essays on the living past. *ISBN 0-86381-371-4; £4.50*
- **THE TALE OF TABUN**
  Nazi chemical weapons in North Wales by Roy Sloan. *ISBN 0-86381-465-4; £5.95*
- **DR WILLAM PRICE - SAINT OR SINNER?**
  - Cyril Bracegirdle. 136 pp. An eccentric and a rebel, William Price left his mark on the history of Wales. *ISBN 0-86381-434-4; £5.75*
- **FIGURES IN A LANDSCAPE**
  A guide to the historical characters of North Wales by Michael Senior.
  Part 1: Maelgwn to Sir John Wyn.
  ISBN 0-86381-469-7
  Part 2: Madocks to Sir Clough Williams-Ellis.
  ISBN 0-86381-488-3;
  116 pp; £5.50 each with maps and black and white illustrations.

ANTHOLOGIES/POETRY/TRAVELLERS IN WALES ▷

- ## AN ANGLESEY ANTHOLOGY
  - Dewi Roberts.
  ISBN 0-86381-566-9; £4.95

- ## THE LAUGHARNE POEMS
  - Thomas Crowe. Poems by the first writer since Dylan Thomas to work from the boat house.
  ISBN 0-86381-432-8; £4.50

- ## SKYWALLS - A SNOWDONIA SEQUENCE
  Poems and paintings by Clyde Holmes.
  ISBN 0-86381-466-2; £5.75

- ## VISITOR'S DELIGHT
  - Dewi Roberts. An anthology of visitor's impressions of North Wales. 152 pp.
  ISBN 0-86381-224-4; £3.75

- ## THE A-Z OF BETWS-Y-COED
  - Donald Shaw. Full of facts, stories and history about the popular Welsh resort. 136 pp.
  ISBN 0-86381-153-1; £2.99

- ## SNOWDONIA, A HISTORICAL ANTHOLOGY
  - David Kirk. 60 writers portray the people and landscape of the one of the most beautiful regions in Europe, 248 pp.
  ISBN 0-86381-270-8; £5.95

- ## ALL THE DAYS WERE GLORIOUS
  - Gwyn Neale. George Gissing in North Wales - quotes from Gissing's letters and diary, 56 pp.
  ISBN 0-86381-286-4; £2.95

- ## THE LAND OF OLD RENOWN - GEORGE BORROW IN WALES
  - Dewi Roberts. A retrace of George Borrow's journey through Wales.
  ISBN 0-86381-436-0; £4.50

- ## BOTH SIDES OF THE BORDER
  An Anthology of writing on the Welsh Border Region by Dewi Roberts.
  ISBN 0-86381-461-1; £4.75

- ## A TOUR IN WALES BY THOMAS PENNANT
  An old classic abridged by David Kirk. 176 pp.
  ISBN 0-86381-473-5; £5.75

- ## REVD JOHN PARKER'S TOUR OF WALES AND ITS CHURCHES (1798-1860)
  Abriged by Edgar W. Parry.
  ISBN 0-86381-481-6; £4.75

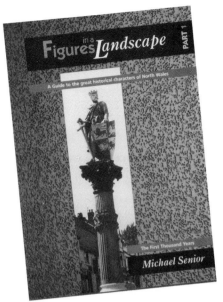

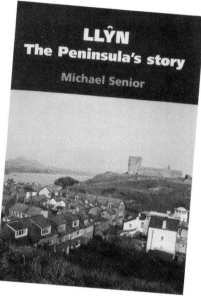

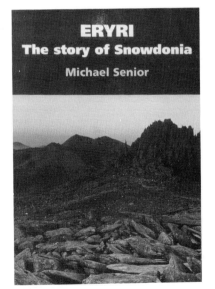

FOLKLORE

- ## SUPERNATURAL CLWYD
  - Richard Holland. A collection of Clwyd's supernatural folktales. 210 pp; many illustrations and photographs.
  ISBN 0-86381-127-2; £4.50

- ## HAUNTED CLWYD
  - Richard Holland. From Clwyd's rich heritage of folklore to present day first-hand accounts, here are phantoms of all descriptions, homely or terrifying. 144 pp; many illustrations.
  ISBN 0-86381-218-X; £3.50

- ## BYE-GONES
  - Richard Holland. Old volumes of Bye-Gones, a periodical published between 1871 and 1939, are a treasure trove of anecdotes relating to Wales and the Border Counties. Black and white illustrations. 120 pp.
  ISBN 0-86381-239-2; £3.50

- ## WELSH GHOSTLY ENCOUNTERS
  - Jane Pugh. A collection of ancient stories and also a few recent accounts of ghostly encounters. 136 pp.
  ISBN 0-86381-152-3; £2.75

- ## WAYS WITH HAZEL AND HORN
  - Bob Griff/Meurig Owen. Traditional stickmaking.
  ISBN 0-86381-367-4; £3.95

- ## RUMOURS AND ODDITIES FROM NORTH WALES
  A selection of folklore, myths & ghost stories - Meirion Hughes and Wayne Evans. A fascinating collection of stories, presenting legends, folk heroes and sinister ghosts. Many illustrations. 112 pp.
  ISBN 0-86381-337-2; £3.00

- ## THE HAUNTING OF GLAMORGAN AND GWENT
  - Russell Gascoigne. This book records numerous examples of other wordly phenomena - tales of shipwrecks, pirates and smugglers, of haunted castles, crumbling ruins and remote farmhouses. Many illustrations; 104 pp.
  ISBN 0-86381-262-7; £3.75

- ## TALES OF OLD GLAMORGAN
  - Wendy Hughes. In this book, Wendy Hughes brings alive the tales which lie at the heart of the county of Glamorgan - legends, fables of fairies and magic, as well as stories of devils, witches and ghosts. Black and white illustrations. 132 pp.
  ISBN 0-86381-287-2; £4.25

- ## GODS AND HEROES IN NORTH WALES - A MYTHOLOGICAL GUIDE
  - Michael Senior. Here, the author deals with the true mythology of Britain, some important parts of which are located in North Wales. Black and white illustrations. 96 pp.
  ISBN 0-86381-249-X; £3.25

- ## COUNTRY CHURCHYARDS IN WALES
  - Donald Gregory. Including maps and illustrations.
  ISBN 0-86381-183-3; £3.50

- ## CELTIC HIGH CROSSES OF WALES
  - John Sharkey.
  ISBN 0-86381-489-1; £5.75

- ## WELSH MYSTERY AND MAGIC
  - Donald Gregory.
  ISBN 0-86381-561-8; £4.75